KERRY LORD

HOW TO CROCHET ANIMALS
OCEAN
25 MINI MENAGERIE PATTERNS

LARK
New York

CONTENTS

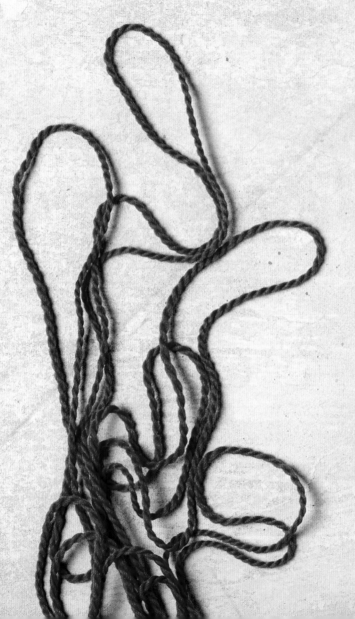

INTRODUCTION

I hope this book will not only be a brilliant introduction to crochet for anyone picking up a hook for the first time but also give a lot of enjoyment to anyone already familiar with the single crochet stitch. I believe learning to crochet is something that should be done with the clear motivation of a pattern to master and the resulting feeling of accomplishment when that project is complete. These quick and easy crochet animals are a great way to start to learn a range of basic and more advanced crochet techniques, and the variety of projects and progression of difficulty across the twenty-five patterns should keep even a seasoned maker entertained and challenged.

I learned to crochet from a video that taught me the US single crochet stitch (British "double crochet"). As with anything new, holding a hook and yarn felt awkward and unfamiliar, but even after just a few hours of perseverance I found my way of holding the hook and working the stitches and discovered how much fun you could have with just one simple technique. This book is gathers together all of my experience learning to crochet and teaching people to crochet over the last eight years. I am completely humbled by the idea that through the Edward's Menagerie pattern series I have not only been able to teach thousands of people face to face to crochet through workshops and events but have also inspired millions of people worldwide with all my books and TOFT video tutorials. Learning to crochet completely changed my life, and I hope I can share the happiness mastering this hobby has brought me as far and wide as possible.

TOFT is a company I started fourteen years ago with no idea what it would grow to become. Our vision is to enrich the lives of as many people as possible with our shared love of craft, and our mission is to be as creative and original as possible and make products to inspire that in others. We specialize in luxury natural yarns and quality long-lasting tools that come together in your hands to give you the pleasure of making the stitches and spreading happiness with the results of your time.

I've tried to capture some of the ocean's most popular animals with a real variety of shapes and species from fish to mammals and crustaceans. I hope you enjoy a little journey around the world and discover some new favorites as you hook your way through the collection. This book of mini patterns forms part of a series also including *Wild*, *Farm*, and *Pets*, so once you've enjoyed crocheting a few dozen sardines you might want to turn your hands to an elephant or maybe a puppy or two.

For me, crochet is bit of a counterpoint to the busy rhythm and routine of my life. It allows me to feel creative after a long day that might have otherwise felt very mundane, and these mini animals make brilliant gifts for friends and family without being too much of an investment in materials or time. Although it may be slower when you are starting out, once you've got a couple of techniques under your belt, these mini patterns are the perfect size to make in an evening. So, when you've got a craft itch to scratch, grab a hook, a handful of your favorite yarn, and carve out a few hours to relax and enjoy the mindfulness of the single crochet stitch and the focus and rewards it brings.

HOW TO USE THIS BOOK

The projects in this book are arranged in order of difficulty, with their corresponding techniques and new skills detailed when they are introduced.

If you are learning to crochet, then start at the beginning of the book and turn each page, reading all the tips and tricks, and trying a few of the exercises to get you used to holding your hook and yarn before you dive into your first project.

If you are already a confident crocheter then start with whatever strikes your fancy and dip in and out of the projects. If you hit an abbreviation or instruction you are unsure of and would like to refresh your understanding then use the technique index on page 109 to find the full step-by-step breakdown.

All the standard stuffing and sewing up details can be found on page 29; follow these guidelines unless instructed otherwise. Unless otherwise stated in the pattern, once you have worked the last round of each pattern piece, gather the stitches when fastening off a part using the technique detailed on page 16.

I have used American English crochet terms throughout. "Single crochet" (sc) is the same as the British English "double crochet" (dc). For clarification of which stitch this refers to, please see the basic instruction for the sc stitch on page 15.

TOFT

All the projects in this book are created using TOFT pure wool double knitting yarn on a C2 (3 mm) aluminium hook with a pure wool stuffing. I have had the pleasure of selecting, designing, and manufacturing luxury yarns for the past fourteen years as the founder of the TOFT brand, and Edward's Menagerie has been inspired by this range of yarns. TOFT yarns are luxury, quality, natural fibers manufactured to my distinctive specifications here in the UK. When crocheted in TOFT yarns, the projects in this book are supple and soft but have a closed fabric to hide the stuffing inside.

Using natural fibers is not only better for the environment but also ensures a beautiful finish, assures you that these animals will only get better over time, and guarantees each stitch is a pleasure to make.

TOFT is here to help if you are new to crochet and not sure where to begin, and the brand is based in a real place called Toft in Warwickshire, England. In addition to our yarns, TOFT now designs and manufactures a whole range of tools and accessories to accompany the Edward's Menagerie crochet range. Video help is on hand if you are struggling at any point with the techniques in this book. All materials, kits, and videos for these projects are available at **www.toftuk.com**.

ESSENTIAL TOOLS

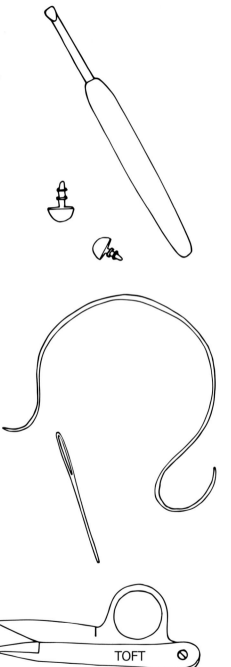

HOOK

Choose the right sized hook to match your yarn and create the correct gauge (see page 11). If you're buying a hook for the first time, get a good-quality one with a comfortable handle as it also doubles as the perfect tool for placing the toy stuffing inside small parts.

STITCH MARKER

Marking the start or end of your rounds when working this style of crochet is essential. I recommend using a piece of contrast yarn, approximately 6 inches (15 cm) long, positioned in the last stitch of Round 2. As you return back around to your marker, pull it forward or backward through or between your stitches to mark the end of the round you have just finished to help you keep track of where you are in the pattern. The marker will weave up the fabric with you, and you can simply pull it free to remove it at the end. Should you ever need to abandon your crochet halfway through a round of instruction, or if you simply lose your place when counting, you will be able to return to your marker and thus never have to do a total restart.

SCISSORS

Sharper scissors may be required for trimming the knot lengths on the prawn.

STUFFING

You can use a natural or man-made stuffing material inside your animals. Using polyester stuffing will make them easier to wash by hand or in a cool cycle in the machine.

SEWING NEEDLE

Ensure your sewing needle has a big enough eye to make it easy to thread with your chosen yarn.

CONTRAST YARN OR SAFETY EYES

I have used black yarn to sew on all of the animals' eyes and noses. Although safety eyes could be added before sewing up, please be aware that these should not be used on a toy for a child under five years of age.

EXTRA TOOLS

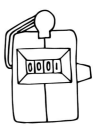

ROW COUNTER
Use a row counter if following a pattern is a new discipline for you. It may make it easier to keep track of the pattern if you do not wish to mark your place in the book.

PROJECT BAG
Although not essential, a project bag can be very handy to keep your latest project safe and in order, especially if you are transporting your crochet with you on a commute or to make the most of your lunch break.

PINS FOR SEWING UP
If you are new to making "3-D" crochet, then pins might help you position all the parts before sewing them together. While not essential, they can come in handy if you know that sewing eyes and ears onto the faces poses a challenge for your perfectionism.

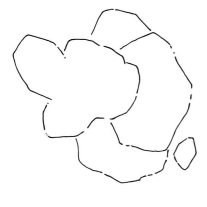

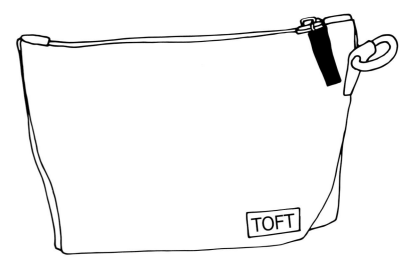

YARN

I was inspired to learn to crochet and make these patterns by TOFT yarn, and all of the creatures in this book have been created in TOFT's pure wool double knitting (DK) yarn using a C2 (3 mm) hook. Each animal takes around ½–¾ ounces (18–22 g) of TOFT yarn and the finished height/ length is 4 inches (10 cm).

TOFT DK pure wool yarn comes in a spectrum of twelve natural colors and twelve bright colors. You can see the bright colors on the tentacles opposite, and the naturals from the top are: Cream, Silver, Shale, Steel, Charcoal, Oatmeal, Stone, Camel, Fudge, Chestnut, Mushroom, and Cocoa.

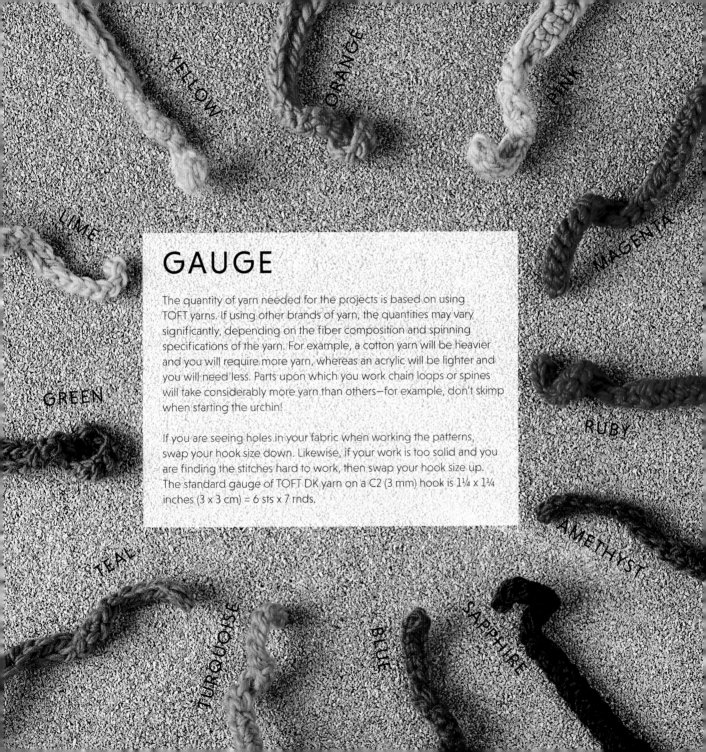

GAUGE

The quantity of yarn needed for the projects is based on using TOFT yarns. If using other brands of yarn, the quantities may vary significantly, depending on the fiber composition and spinning specifications of the yarn. For example, a cotton yarn will be heavier and you will require more yarn, whereas an acrylic will be lighter and you will need less. Parts upon which you work chain loops or spines will take considerably more yarn than others—for example, don't skimp when starting the urchin!

If you are seeing holes in your fabric when working the patterns, swap your hook size down. Likewise, if your work is too solid and you are finding the stitches hard to work, then swap your hook size up. The standard gauge of TOFT DK yarn on a C2 (3 mm) hook is 1¼ x 1¼ inches (3 x 3 cm) = 6 sts x 7 rnds.

HOLDING YOUR HOOK

There are two principal ways of holding your crochet hook, one similar to holding a knife and the other to holding a pencil. If you are totally new to crochet, I would recommend the knife hold as easier to get comfortable with and maintain control and a good tension, but if you already use the pencil hold successfully, then do not alter it. Even within these two holds there are lots of subtle variants on how to hold your hook and there is no wrong or right way. Do what is most comfortable for you.

Knife hold

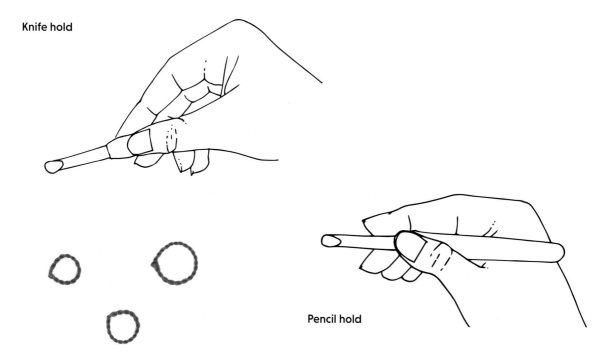

Pencil hold

HOLDING YOUR YARN

Every crocheter I meet holds their yarn in a slightly different way, so use these illustrations as a rough guide and then experiment with what's most comfortable for you. Only adjust your hand position if you think the way you hold the yarn is causing a problem: loose stitches can be caused by not putting tension onto the yarn coming off the ball by wrapping it around your finger, but the opposite problem of the yarn not moving freely can often be worse and you will feel like you are fighting the stitches and creating a very tight gauge.

If you are left-handed, there are no special changes you need to make as none of the patterns in this book refers to left and right.

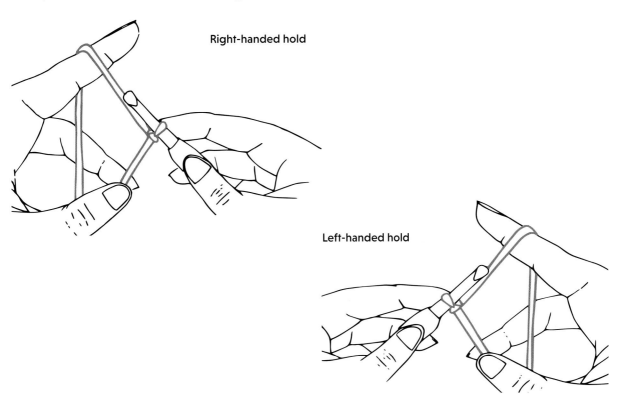

Right-handed hold

Left-handed hold

LEARNING TO CROCHET

Practice your hook and hand positions from the previous pages by working a long chain length. It will get you used to coordinating both hands and finding what works best for you. If you are comfortable working the stitches and achieving the correct gauge, there is no wrong or right.

SLIP KNOT

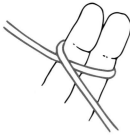

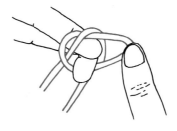

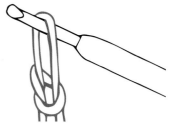

1 Wrap the yarn around your fingers.

2 Pull the tail end of the yarn through the wrap to make a loop.

3 Place your hook through the loop and tighten, ensuring that it is the tail end of the yarn (not the ball end) that controls the opening and closing of the knot.

CHAIN (CH)

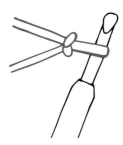

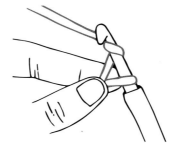

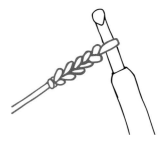

1 Make a slip knot.

2 Wrap the yarn over the hook (yarn over) and pull it through the loop on the hook.

3 Repeat until desired length.

SINGLE CROCHET STITCH (SC)

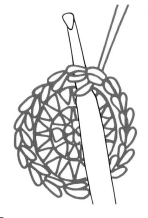

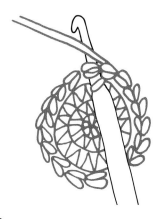

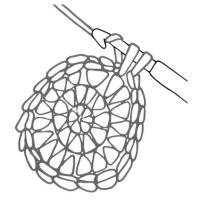

1 Insert the hook through the stitch under both loops of the "V" unless otherwise stated.

2 Yarn over, rotate hook head, and pull through the stitch (two loops on hook).

3 Yarn over again and pull through both loops on the hook to end with one loop on the hook (one single crochet stitch made).

SC6 INTO RING (MAGIC CIRCLE)

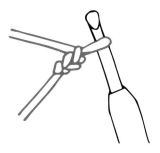

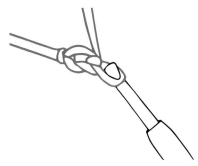

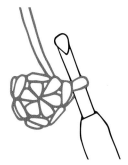

1 Make a slip knot and chain two stitches.

2 Insert the hook into the first chain stitch made and work a single crochet six times into this same stitch.

3 Pull tightly on the tail of the yarn to close the center of the ring and form a neat circle.

DECREASING (SC2TOG)

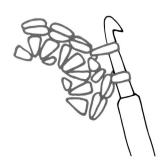

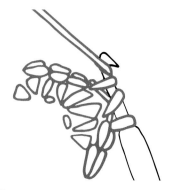

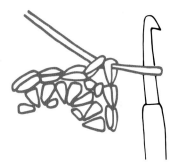

1   Insert the hook under the front loop only of the next stitch (two loops on hook).

2   In the same motion, insert the hook through the front loop only of the following stitch (three loops on hook).

3   Yarn over and pull through the first two loops on the hook, then yarn over and pull through both remaining loops to complete the single crochet decrease. See page 17 for the completed stitch.

FASTENING OFF

Once you have finished a piece, you'll need to fasten off the yarn to secure it so the stitch does not unravel.

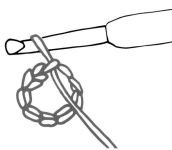

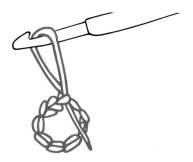

1   When finishing the last stitch of any round, simply cut the yarn, leaving 3–4 inches (8–10 cm) for sewing up.

2   Pull your hook upward away from your work until the end goes through the loop on hook.

3   Pull to tighten.

COUNTING YOUR STITCHES

An essential skill to keep yourself on track and able to follow the pattern accurately is knowing how to count the number of stitches you have in a round. While learning, count your stitches in a round after each line of pattern that involves increasing or decreasing. The number in brackets at the end of a line in the pattern indicates the number of stitches you should have once it is completed. If you complete a round and this number is wrong, then pull back your work to the beginning of the round and redo it until you have the correct number of stitches before you progress—this is much easier with a stitch marker (see page 8).

COUNTING A CHAIN
When you crochet a chain and then work back down it, you will often miss the stitch closest to the hook in order to turn. For example, you might chain ten stitches in order to single crochet nine stitches back down the chain.

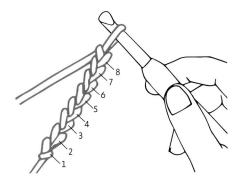

COUNTING THE STITCHES IN A ROUND
The majority of the time your crochet piece will grow from a set number of stitches in a closed ring (usually six). The piece you are making grows because you are increasing the number of stitches by sometimes working two single crochet into the same stitch as instructed.

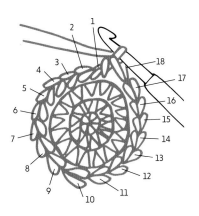

READING A PATTERN AND ABBREVIATIONS

STS: STITCHES
The number in brackets at the end of a line indicates the number of stitches in that round once it has been completed.

RND: ROUND
A round is a complete rotation in a spiral back to where you started. In this style of crochet, you DO NOT slip stitch at the end of a round to make a circle, but instead continue directly on to the next round in a spiral.

Begin by sc6 into ring

Rnd 1 (sc2 into next st) 6 times (12 sts)

Rnd 2 (sc1, sc2 into next st) 6 times (18)

Rnd 3 (sc2, sc2 into next st) 6 times (24)

Rnd 4 (sc3, sc2 into next st) 6 times (30)

Rnd 5 (sc4, sc2 into next st) 6 times (36)

Rnd 6 (sc5, sc2 into next st) 6 times (42)

Rnd 7 (sc6, sc2 into next st) 6 times (48)

Rnds 8–10 sc (3 rnds)

6 TIMES
Repeat what comes directly before this instruction within the brackets the number of times stated.

SC: SINGLE CROCHET
sc5 means to single crochet one stitch into each of the next five stitches.

3 RNDS
Work one single crochet stitch into every stitch in the round for three full rounds.

Additional abbreviations
ch: chain
sc2tog: single crochet two stitches together
   (to turn two stitches into one and
   decrease a round count by one stitch)
sl st: slip stitch

BASICS OF
SPIRAL CROCHET

When working the style of crochet used in this book to create a solid fabric and "3-D" shapes, you generally start from a closed ring and work the single crochet stitch in one direction in a nonstop spiral. The pattern on page 18 forms a pretty standard increase for this style of crochet by adding six stitches evenly into every round. The piece becomes "3-D" once you stop adding six stitches into a round.

RIGHT SIDE (RS) AND WRONG SIDE (WS)

If you are new to this style of crochet, you do need to be aware that there is a right side (RS) and wrong side (WS) to the fabric; the wrong side forms the inside of the shape. If you are right-handed and crocheting with the RS facing outward, you will be moving in counterclockwise direction around the edge of the circle of fabric (left-handed people will be moving clockwise). It is very easy to have learned to crochet holding the WS facing outward (I did it myself); this will mean that your resulting piece will be inside out when you come to stuff and finish it. With some parts, this will not be a problem, as you can simply flip them before stuffing and sewing up. However, with the parts containing smaller rounds, such as tails, this will be impossible, so it is best to adjust your hold to ensure you are crocheting into the right side of the fabric, with this on the outside of the "3-D" shape. On the right side of the fabric, you will see the rounds horizontally on the piece. On the wrong side, you can see vertical furrows spiralling up the piece.

STUFFING USING BACK OF HOOK

The majority of "3-D" shapes you are crocheting will need stuffing, and this can be done at the end unless otherwise stated. Using TOFT pure wool produces a fabric that is forgiving and supple, and this combines really well with light-handed stuffing to create animals that feel soft to the touch rather than dense or stiff. You want to show off the shaping within the piece, not overstuff it until the shape is lost and the stuffing shows through the stitches. My advice would be that less is better.

Follow the pattern opposite to practice your single crochet stitches before starting your first animal. Once you feel more familiar with the stitch on this bigger piece, it will be easier to work the smaller rounds required in many of the minis.

JELLYFISH

BODY/HEAD
Begin by sc6 into ring.
Rnd 1 (sc2 into next st) 6 times (12 sts)
Rnd 2 (sc1, sc2 into next st) 6 times (18)
Rnd 3 (sc2, sc2 into next st) 6 times (24)
Rnd 4 (sc3, sc2 into next st) 6 times (30)
Rnd 5 sc
Rnd 6 (sc4, sc2 into next st) 6 times (36)
Rnds 7–8 sc (2 rnds)
Rnd 9 (sc5, sc2 into next st) 6 times (42)
Rnds 10–12 sc (3 rnds)

BASE
Begin by sc6 into ring.
Rnd 1 (sc2 into next st) 6 times (12)
Rnd 2 (sc1, sc2 into next st) 6 times (18)
Rnd 3 (sc2, sc2 into next st) 6 times (24)
Rnd 4 (sc3, sc2 into next st) 6 times (30)
Rnd 5 (sc4, sc2 into next st) 6 times (36)
Rnd 6 (sc5, sc2 into next st) 6 times (42)
Stuff and attach body/head to base with a rnd of sc
  through both edges from the bottom upward, ensuring
  right sides are facing out.

TENTACLES (make three)
Work three ch30 SLIP STITCH CHAINS (see page 22) into
  center of base.

ARMS (make three)
Sl st into center of base, ch30, turn, and sc2 into every stitch
  back down ch, sl st into base to secure (60).
Repeat for each arm.

Finish by sewing eyes into place with Black yarn.

This is a great place to start as you are just
growing the piece out from the initial ring
without any decreasing.

SLIP STITCH CHAINS

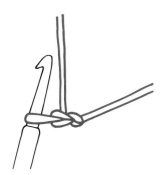
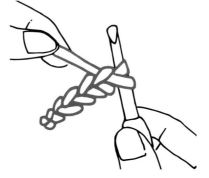

1 Insert the hook through the fabric at the desired position, yarn over, and pull through the fabric.

2 Chain the number of stitches stated in the pattern.

3 Working back down the chain, insert the hook into the next stitch, yarn over, and pull through the stitch and the loop on the hook (one slip stitch made). Continue slip stitching down the chain, ending with just one loop on the hook.

CROCHETING TWO PIECES TOGETHER

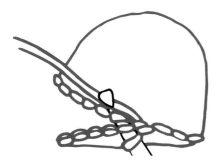

Join the pieces by working sc through both edges, in this instance working from the bottom upward, right sides facing out.

SEWING ON EYES/NOSTRILS

1. Secure the yarn to the fabric at the top of the desired eye (or nostril) position.
2. Sew down through the fabric around one stitch.
3. Move through the inside of the piece and repeat for the second eye (or nostril). Secure and trim the ends.

If using safety eyes, don't forget to add them before gathering your stitches but after stuffing. The character of your animal is dictated by the position of its facial features and most importantly the eyes. A face with larger eyes will look cuter, and adding two very simple nostrils can suddenly add the finishing touch.

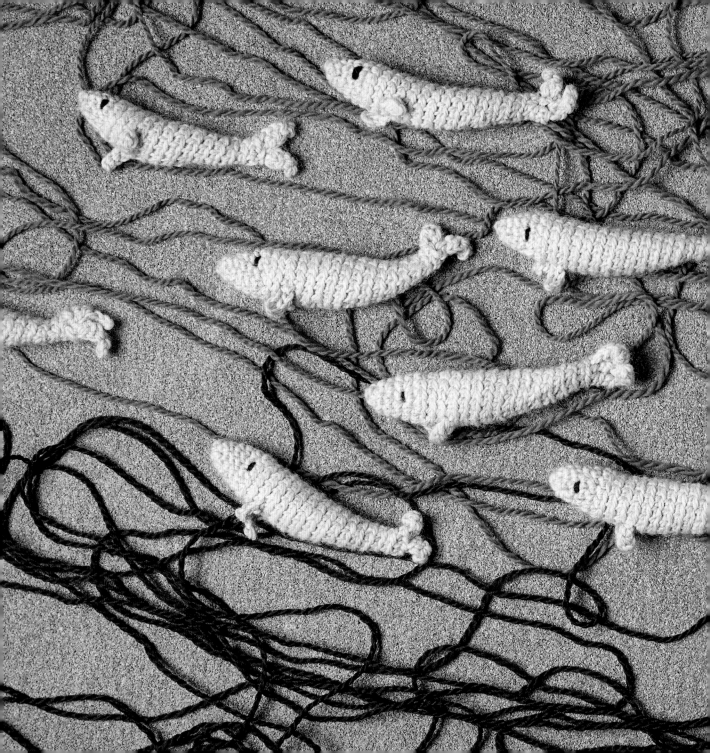

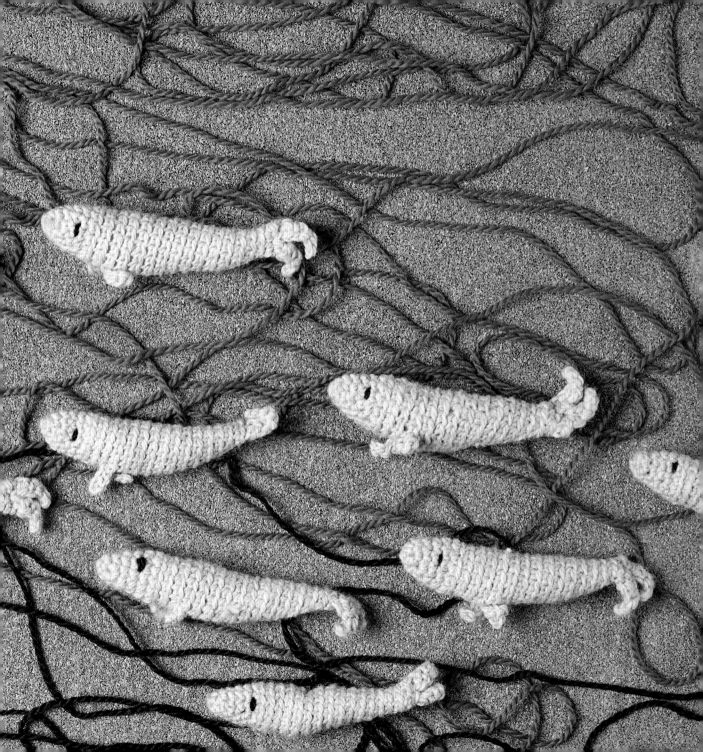

SARDINES

HEAD/BODY
Begin by sc4 into ring.
Rnd 1 (sc2 into next st, sc1) twice (6 sts)
Rnd 2 (sc2 into next st, sc2) twice (8)
Rnd 3 (sc2 into next st, sc3) twice (10)
Rnd 4 sc
Rnd 5 (sc2 into next st, sc4) twice (12)
Rnd 6 sc2 into next st, sc11 (13)
Continue working into back loops only.
Rnds 7–8 sc (2 rnds)
Rnd 9 sc2 into next st, sc12 (14)
Rnds 10–11 sc (2 rnds)
Rnd 12 sc2tog, sc12 (13)
Rnd 13 sc
Rnd 14 sc2tog, sc11 (12)
Rnd 15 sc2tog, sc10 (11)
Rnd 16 sc2tog, sc9 (10)
Rnd 17 sc2tog, sc8 (9)
Rnd 18 sc2tog, sc7 (8)
Rnd 19 sc2tog, sc6 (7)
Stuff and continue.
Rnd 20 sc2tog, sc5 (6)
Rnd 21 sc
Continue to tail.

TAIL
Ch5, turn, and work back down ch as follows:
sl st1, sc2, hdc1.
Sl st into center of tail through both edges of the rnd, then
ch5, turn, and work back down ch as above, sl st into
base of tail to secure.

FINS (make two)
Work two ch5 SLIP STITCH CHAINS (see page 22) into
position.

Finish by sewing eyes into place with Black yarn.

This is great for learning to decrease and
working into the back loop only.

WORKING INTO BACK LOOPS ONLY

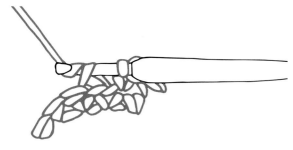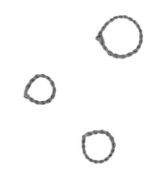

Insert the hook in between the two strands of the "V" of the next stitch so that you are working under the back loop only. This leaves the front loop to form a lined texture on the surface of the right side of the fabric.

HALF DOUBLE CROCHET STITCH (HDC)

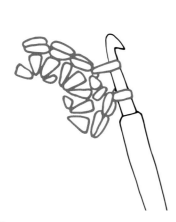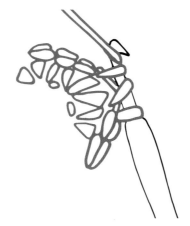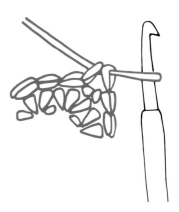

1 Yarn over and insert the hook into the next stitch.

2 Yarn over and pull through the stitch (three loops on hook).

3 Yarn over and pull through all three loops on the hook (one half double crochet stitch made).

OCTOPUS

MANTLE/HEAD
Begin by sc6 into ring.
Rnd 1 (sc2 into next st) 6 times (12 sts)
Rnd 2 (sc1, sc2 into next st) 6 times (18)
Rnd 3 (sc2, sc2 into next st) 6 times (24)
Rnd 4 (sc3, sc2 into next st) 6 times (30)
Rnd 5 (sc4, sc2 into next st) 6 times (36)
Rnds 6–8 sc (3 rnds)
Rnd 9 (sc1, sc2tog) 6 times, sc18 (30)
Rnds 10–11 sc (2 rnds)
Rnd 12 (sc3, sc2tog) 6 times (24)
Rnds 13–14 sc (2 rnds)
Rnd 15 (sc6, sc2tog) 3 times (21)
Rnd 16 sc
Rnd 17 (sc2, sc2 into next st) 7 times (28)
Rnds 18–19 sc (2 rnds)
Rnd 20 (sc6, sc2 into next st) 4 times (32)

BASE
Begin by sc6 into ring.
Rnd 1 (sc2 into next st) 6 times (12)
Rnd 2 (sc1, sc2 into next st) 6 times (18)
Rnd 3 (sc2, sc2 into next st) 6 times (24)
Rnd 4 (sc2, sc2 into next st) 8 times (32)
Stuff and attach mantle/head to base with a rnd of sc
 through both edges from the top down, ensuring right
 sides are facing out.

TENTACLES (make eight)
Working around join between mantle/head and base,
 sl st into position.
Ch25 and work back down ch as follows:
skip first st, sl st6, sc6, hdc6, dc6.
Skip 3 sts along bottom of body, sl st1, and repeat 7 times
 more.

EYES (make two)
Begin by sc6 into ring.
Rnd 1 (sc1, sc2 into next st) 3 times (9)

Finish by sewing pupils onto the eyes with Black yarn.

This is great for learning all the basic crochet stitches.

DOUBLE CROCHET STITCH (DC)

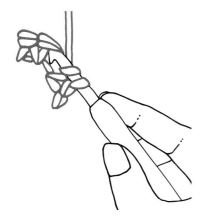 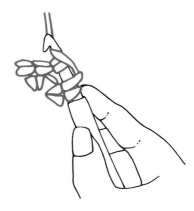 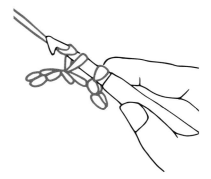

1   Yarn over and insert the hook into the next stitch.

2   Yarn over and pull through the stitch (three loops on hook), then yarn over again, and pull through the first two loops on the hook (two loops on hook).

3   Yarn over again and pull through the remaining two loops on the hook (one double crochet stitch made).

SEWING ON A PIECE

1. Pin if necessary.
2. Backstitch around the edge.
3. Fasten off by sewing through the piece and around a stitch.

URCHIN

BODY

Begin by sc6 into ring.
Rnd 1 (sc2 into next st) 6 times (12 sts)
Rnd 2 (sc1, sc2 into next st) 6 times (18)
Rnd 3 (sc2, sc2 into next st) 6 times (24)
Rnd 4 (sc3, sc2 into next st) 6 times (30)
Rnds 5–10 sc (6 rnds)
Rnd 11 (sc3, sc2tog) 6 times (24)
Rnd 12 (sc2, sc2tog) 6 times (18)
Rnd 13 (sc1, sc2tog) 6 times (12)
Rnd 14 (sc2tog) 6 times (6)

SPINES

Work ch16 SLIP STITCH CHAINS (see page 22) all over
body with 2 SLIP STITCH TRAVERSE sts (see page 35)
between each spine.

Finish by sewing eyes into place with Black yarn.

This is great for mastering surface slip stitch
chains to add texture.

GATHERING STITCHES

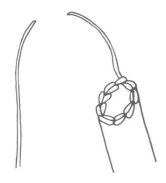
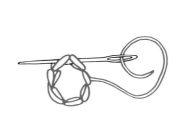

1   Fasten off the last stitch of the round.

2   Thread the end of the yarn onto a sewing needle and sew a running stitch through all the remaining stitches of the round.

3   Pull tightly to gather and close the stitches, then fasten off into the fabric around a stitch.

SLIP STITCH TRAVERSE

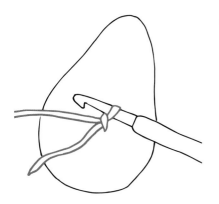
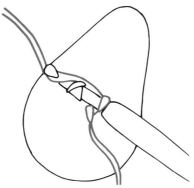
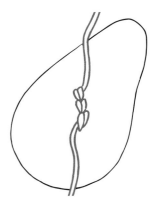

1   Insert the hook into the fabric around a stitch or row.

2   Yarn over and pull through the stitch and all loops on the hook (one slip stitch made).

3   Repeat in desired direction, moving across the surface of the fabric.

PUFFERFISH

BODY/HEAD
Begin by sc6 into ring.
Rnd 1 (sc2 into next st) 6 times (12 sts)
Rnd 2 (sc1, sc2 into next st) 6 times (18)
Rnd 3 (sc2, sc2 into next st) 6 times (24)
Rnd 4 (sc3, sc2 into next st) 6 times (30)
Rnd 5 sc
Rnd 6 (sc4, sc2 into next st) 6 times (36)
Rnds 7–12 sc (6 rnds)
Rnd 13 (sc2tog, sc10) 3 times (33)
Rnd 14 sc
Rnd 15 (sc2tog, sc9) 3 times (30)
Rnd 16 sc
Rnd 17 (sc2tog, sc8) 3 times (27)
Rnd 18 sc
Rnd 19 (sc2tog, sc7) 3 times (24)
Rnd 20 (sc2tog, sc6) 3 times (21)
Rnd 21 (sc2tog, sc5) 3 times (18)
Rnd 22 (sc2tog, sc4) 3 times (15)
Rnd 23 (sc2tog, sc3) 3 times (12)
Rnds 24–25 sc (2 rnds)
Stuff and continue to tail.

TAIL
Fold flat and dc6 across edge to close.
Turn and dc2 into each gap between sts (10.)

FINS (make two)
Sl st into position on body and dc4 into same st.
Turn and dc2 into each gap between sts (6.)

SPINES
Work SLIP STITCH CHAINS (see page 22) from tail toward
   the head with two rotations in each of the chain lengths
   as follows: ch4, ch5, ch6, ch7 and ch8.
Work 2 SLIP STITCH TRAVERSE sts (see page 35) between
   each spine.

MOUTH
Ch12 and sl st to join into a circle.
Rnds 1–2 sc (2 rnds)

Finish by sewing eyes into place with Black yarn.

Bring together everything you've learned
so far and also learn an open chain start as
an alternative to the ring start.

CHAIN AND THEN SLIP STITCH TO JOIN INTO A CIRCLE

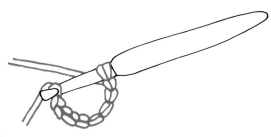

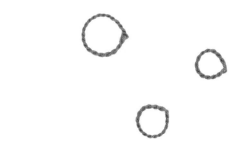

1 Chain the stated number of stitches, then insert the hook into the back of the stitch closest to the slip knot, ensuring not to twist the stitches.

2 Yarn over the hook.

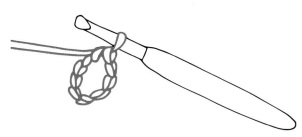

3 Pull the yarn through the stitch and the loop on the hook in one motion.

THE CORAL REEF

Reimagine your favorite patterns in different colors within the natural and bright spectrums to create different species of sea creatures.

SQUID

MANTLE
Begin by sc6 into ring.
Rnd 1 sc
Rnd 2 (sc2 into next st, sc2) twice (8 sts)
Rnd 3 (sc2 into next st, sc3) twice (10)
Rnd 4 (sc2 into next st, sc4) twice (12)
Rnd 5 (sc2 into next st, sc5) twice (14)
Rnd 6 (sc2 into next st, sc6) twice (16)
Rnd 7 (sc2 into next st, sc7) twice (18)
Rnd 8 (sc2 into next st, sc8) twice (20)
Rnd 9 (sc2 into next st, sc9) twice (22)
Rnd 10 (sc2 into next st, sc10) twice (24)
Rnd 11 (sc2 into next st, sc11) twice (26)
Rnd 12 (sc2 into next st, sc12) twice (28)
Rnd 13 (sc2 into next st, sc13) twice (30)
Rnds 14–15 sc (2 rnds)
Rnd 16 (sc3, sc2tog) 6 times (24)
Rnds 17–19 sc (3 rnds)
Rnd 20 (sc3, sc2 into next st) 6 times (30)
Rnd 21 sc
Rnd 22 (sc4, sc2 into next st) 6 times (36)

HEAD
Begin by sc6 into ring.
Rnd 1 (sc2 into next st) 6 times (12)
Rnd 2 sc
Rnd 3 (sc1, sc2 into next st) 6 times (18)
Rnd 4 (sc2, sc2 into next st) 6 times (24)
Rnd 5 (sc3, sc2 into next st) 6 times (30)
Rnd 6 (sc4, sc2 into next st) 6 times (36)
Rnd 7 sc
Stuff and attach mantle to head with a rnd of sc through both edges from the top down, ensuring right sides are facing out.

EYES (make two)
Begin by sc6 into ring.
Rnd 1 (sc1, sc2 into next st) 3 times (9)

ARMS (make eight)
Working around Rnd 3 of head, sl st into position.
Ch20, turn and work back down ch as follows:
sl st4, sc4, hdc4, dc7.
Miss 2 sts along rnd, sl st to secure, and repeat for next arm.

TENTACLES (make two)
Working into center base of head, sl st into position.
Ch44, turn and work back down ch as follows:
sl st2, sc2, hdc2, dc3, hdc2, sc2, sl st30.

FINS (make two)
Right fin: Sl st into position approx. three rnds from top point then work toward head, working sts into mantle as follows:
ch3, dc1, hdc1, sc1, sl st1.
Left fin: Rejoin on opposite side approx. seven rnds from top point and work back up mantle as follows:
sl st1, sc1, hdc1, dc1, ch2, sc1.

Finish by sewing pupils onto the eyes with Black yarn.

STARFISH

BODY/ARMS

Begin by sc6 into ring.
Rnd 1 (sc2 into next st) 6 times (12 sts)
Rnd 2 (sc1, sc2 into next st) 6 times (18)
Rnd 3 (sc2, sc2 into next st) 6 times (24)
Rnd 4 (sc3, sc2 into next st) 6 times (30)
*** Rnd 5** sc6 (incomplete rnd)
Next, ch6, sl st into first sc to form 12-st rnd and work
   as follows:
Rnds 1–5 sc (5 rnds)
Rnd 6 (sc2tog, sc4) twice (10)
Rnds 7–9 sc (3 rnds)
Rnd 10 (sc2tog, sc3) twice (8)
Rnd 11 sc
Rnd 12 (sc2tog) 4 times (4)
Rejoin and repeat from * 4 times more.

BASE

Begin by sc6 into ring.
Rnd 1 (sc2 into next st) 6 times (12)
Rnd 2 (sc1, sc2 into next st) 6 times (18)
Rnd 3 (sc2, sc2 into next st) 6 times (24)
Rnd 4 (sc3, sc2 into next st) 6 times (30)
Rnd 5 (sc5, sc2 into next st) 5 times (35)
Stuff arms and body and attach to base with a rnd of sc
   through both edges from bottom upward by working
   6 sts around the base and through ch sts on each arm,
   and 1 st in between each arm (35).

Finish by sewing eyes into place with Black yarn.

Learn to split larger rounds into smaller ones.

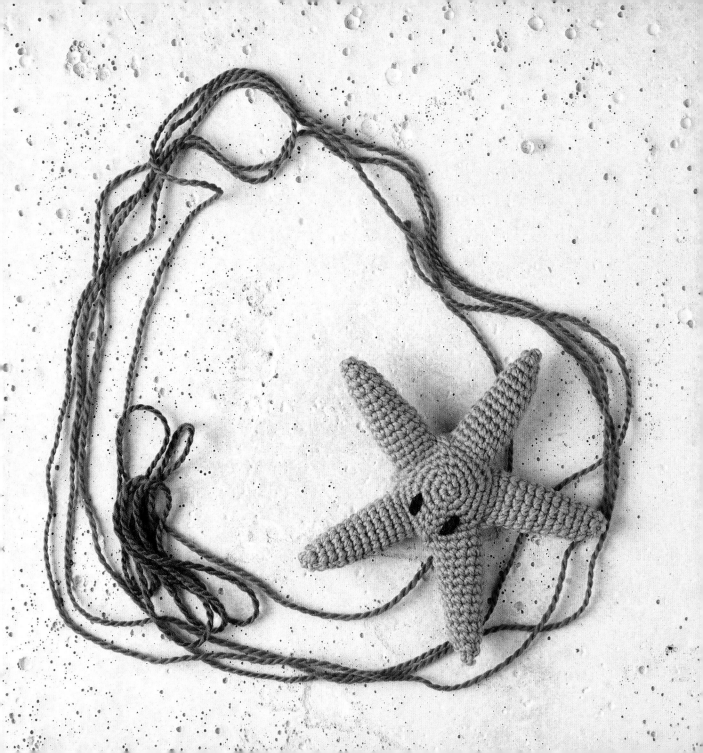

USING A CHAIN TO SPLIT THE ROUND

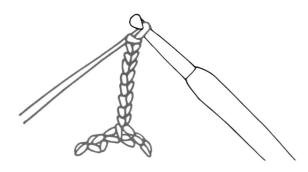

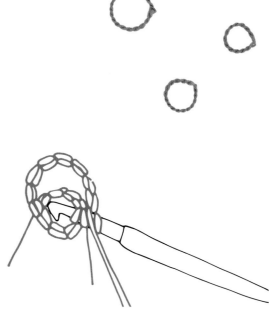

1   Chain the specified number of stitches from your current stitch.

2   Insert the hook from the right side of the fabric through the specified stitch on the original round and slip stitch to join. The chain splits off the specified number of stitches from the original round and forms a new round with them.

3   Work the new round as instructed, then rejoin the yarn to the next stitch along the original round and continue with the pattern. For the starfish, you will be splitting the original round into five smaller rounds to form the arms.

SEA TURTLE

TOP SHELL

Ch6

Rnd 1 sc4, sc2 into next st along one side of chain, sc4, sc2 into next st along other side of chain (12 sts)

Rnd 2 sc2 into next st, sc4, (sc2 into next st) twice, sc4, sc2 into next st (16)

Rnd 3 (sc2 into next st) twice, sc4, (sc2 into next st) 4 times, sc4, (sc2 into next st) twice (24)

Rnd 4 sc2, sc2 into next st, sc6, sc2 into next st, sc4, sc2 into next st, sc6, sc2 into next st, sc2 (28)

Rnd 5 sc1, sc2 into next st, sc2, sc2 into next st, sc4, (sc2 into next st, sc2) 3 times, sc2 into next st, sc4, sc2 into next st, sc2, sc2 into next st, sc1 (36)

Rnds 6–7 sc (2 rnds)

BOTTOM SHELL

Ch6

Rnd 1 sc4, sc2 into next st along one side of chain, sc4, sc2 into next st along other side of chain (12)

Rnd 2 sc2 into next st, sc4, (sc2 into next st) twice, sc4, sc2 into next st (16)

Rnd 3 (sc2 into next st) twice, sc4, (sc2 into next st) 4 times, sc4, (sc2 into next st) twice (24)

Rnd 4 sc2, sc2 into next st, sc6, sc2 into next st, sc4, sc2 into next st, sc6, sc2 into next st, sc2 (28)

Rnd 5 sc1, sc2 into next st, sc2, sc2 into next st, sc4, (sc2 into next st, sc2) 3 times, sc2 into next st, sc4, sc2 into next st, sc2, sc2 into next st, sc1 (36)

Rnd 6 sc

Stuff and attach top shell to bottom shell with a rnd of sc through both edges from bottom upward, ensuring right sides are facing out.

HEAD

Ch8 and sl st to join into a circle.

Rnds 1–2 sc (2 rnds)

Rnd 3 (sc2 into next st, sc2, sc2 into next st) twice (12)

Rnd 4 (sc2 into next st) twice, sc2, (sc2 into next st) 3 times, sc4, sc2 into next st (18)

Rnds 5–6 sc (2 rnds)

Rnd 7 (sc2tog) 6 times, sc6 (12)

Rnd 8 (sc2tog) 3 times, sc6 (9)

FRONT FLIPPERS (make two)

Ch8 and sl st to join into a circle.

Rnds 1–4 sc (4 rnds)

Rnd 5 (sc2tog) twice, (sc2 into next st) 4 times (10)

Rnds 6–9 sc (4 rnds)

Rnd 10 (sc2tog, sc3) twice (8)

Rnds 11–12 sc (2 rnds)

Rnd 13 (sc2tog, sc2) twice (6)

Rnd 14 sc

Rnd 15 (sc2tog) 3 times (3)

Do not stuff.

BACK FLIPPERS (make two)

Ch8 and sl st to join into a circle.

Rnd 1 sc

Rnd 2 (sc2 into next st, sc3) twice (10)

Rnds 3–5 sc (3 rnds)

Rnd 6 (sc2tog) 5 times (5)

Do not stuff.

Finish by sewing eyes into place with Black yarn.

This project is good for learning two different kinds of starts to create an oval shape.

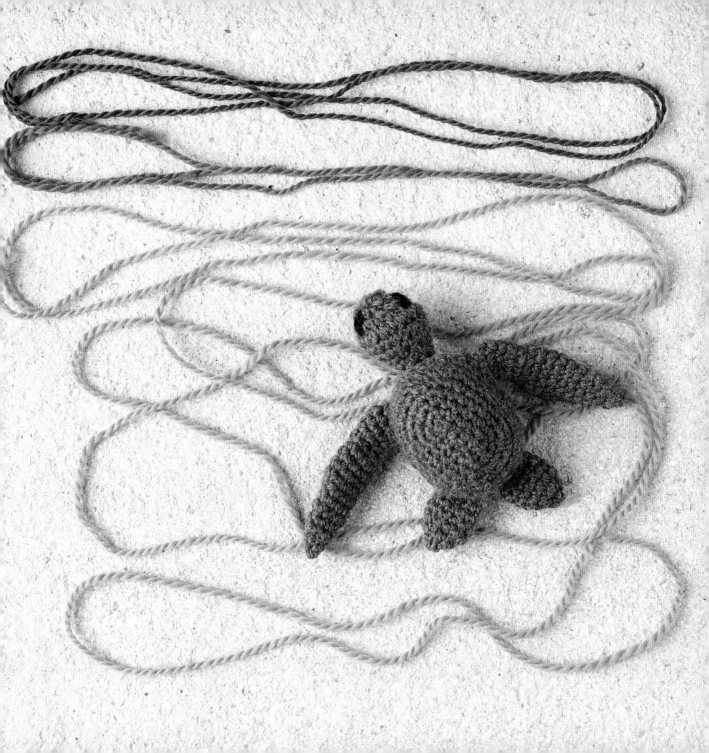

WORKING INTO BOTH SIDES OF A CHAIN TO START A ROUND

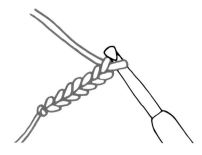

1 Chain the specified number of stitches.

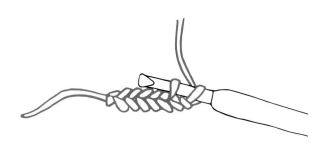

2 Work the first stitch of the round into the second chain from the hook.

3 Continue working down the first side of the chain as instructed, then turn and work back up the other side of the chain to complete the first round. Place a marker.

CRAB

TOP SHELL

Ch6

Rnd 1 sc4, sc2 into next st along one side of chain, sc4, sc2 into next st along other side of chain (12 sts)

Rnd 2 sc2 into next st, sc4, (sc2 into next st) twice, sc4, sc2 into next st (16)

Rnd 3 (sc2 into next st) twice, sc4, (sc2 into next st) 4 times, sc4, (sc2 into next st) twice (24)

Rnd 4 sc2, sc2 into next st, sc6, sc2 into next st, sc4, sc2 into next st, sc6, sc2 into next st, sc2 (28)

Rnd 5 sc1, sc2 into next st, sc2, sc2 into next st, sc4, (sc2 into next st, sc2) 3 times, sc2 into next st, sc4, sc2 into next st, sc2, sc2 into next st, sc1 (36)

Rnds 6–7 sc (2 rnds)

BOTTOM SHELL

Ch6

Rnd 1 sc4, sc2 into next st along one side of chain, sc4, sc2 into next st along other side of chain (12)

Rnd 2 sc2 into next st, sc4, (sc2 into next st) twice, sc4, sc2 into next st (16)

Rnd 3 (sc2 into next st) twice, sc4, (sc2 into next st) 4 times, sc4, (sc2 into next st) twice (24)

Rnd 4 sc2, sc2 into next st, sc6, sc2 into next st, sc4, sc2 into next st, sc6, sc2 into next st, sc2 (28)

Rnd 5 sc1, sc2 into next st, sc2, sc2 into next st, sc4, (sc2 into next st, sc2) 3 times, sc2 into next st, sc4, sc2 into next st, sc2, sc2 into next st, sc1 (36)

Rnd 6 sc

Stuff and attach top shell to bottom shell with a rnd of sc through both edges from bottom upward, ensuring right sides are facing out.

CLAWS (make two)

Begin by sc6 into ring.

Rnd 1 (sc2 into next st) 6 times (12)

Rnds 2–6 sc (5 rnds)

Split into two 6-st rnds and work each as follows:

Rnd 1 sc

Rnd 2 sc2tog, sc4 (5)

Rnd 3 sc2tog, sc3 (4)

Rnd 4 sc1, sc3tog (2)

LEGS (make six)

Begin by sc6 into ring.

Rnds 1–4 sc (4 rnds)

Do not stuff.

EYES (make two)

Begin by sc6 into ring.

Rnds 1–2 sc (2 rnds)

Do not stuff.

Finish by sewing pupils onto the eyes with Black yarn.

SPLITTING THE ROUND

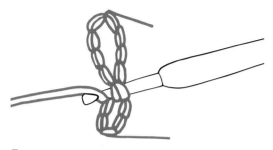

1 Count back the required number of stitches from your hook to split the round as instructed in the pattern. Cross the round and single crochet into this stitch from the right side of the fabric to create two smaller rounds.

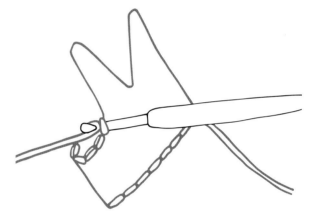

2 Work the stitches on the first smaller round as instructed. Once completed, rejoin the yarn and work the second smaller round.

LOBSTER

BODY/HEAD
Ch6
Rnd 1 sc4, sc2 into next st along one side of chain,
 sc4, sc2 into next st along other side of chain (12 sts)
Rnd 2 sc2 into next st, sc4, (sc2 into next st) twice,
 sc4, sc2 into next st (16)
Rnd 3 sc2 into next st, sc6, (sc2 into next st) twice,
 sc6, sc2 into next st (20)
Rnds 4–11 sc (8 rnds)
Rnd 12 (sc3, sc2tog) 4 times (16)
Rnd 13 sc
Rnd 14 (sc2, sc2tog) 4 times (12)
Rnds 15–17 sc (3 rnds)
Rnd 18 (sc1, sc2 into next st) 6 times (18)
Rnd 19 ch2, dc18
Rnd 20 dc14, hdc2, sc1
Stuff, then fold flat and sc across edge to close.

CLAWS (make two)
Ch6 and sl st to join into a circle.
Rnds 1–4 sc (4 rnds)
Rnd 5 (sc2 into next st) 6 times (12)
Rnds 6–10 sc (5 rnds)
Split into two rnds of 6 sts and rejoin and work each
 as follows:
Rnd 1 sc
Rnd 2 sc2tog, sc4 (5)
Rnd 3 sc2tog, sc3 (4)
Rnd 4 sc1, sc3tog (2)

LEGS (make eight)
Begin by sc5 into ring.
Rnds 1–5 sc (5 rnds)
Do not stuff.

ANTENNAE (make two)
Work two ch12 SLIP STITCH CHAINS (see page 22) into
 top of head.

Finish by sewing eyes into place with Black yarn.

SEA SLUG

BODY
Begin by sc6 into ring.
Rnd 1 (sc2 into next st) 6 times (12 sts)
Rnd 2 (sc1, sc2 into next st) 6 times (18)
Rnds 3–7 sc (5 rnds)
Rnd 8 (sc1, sc2tog) 6 times (12)
Rnds 9–13 sc (5 rnds)
Rnd 14 (sc2, sc2tog) 3 times (9)
Rnds 15–19 sc (5 rnds)
Rnd 20 (sc1, sc2tog) 3 times (6)
Rnds 21–22 sc (2 rnds)

FOOT
Ch12 and sl st to join into a circle.
Rnd 1 sc2 into next st, sc4, (sc2 into next st) twice, sc4, sc2 into next st (16)
Rnd 2 (sc2 into next st) twice, sc4, (sc2 into next st) 4 times, sc4, (sc2 into next st) twice (24)
Rnd 3 sc2, sc2 into next st, sc6, sc2 into next st, sc4, sc2 into next st, sc6, sc2 into next st, sc2 (28)
Rnd 4 [(sc2 into next st) 3 times, sc10, sc2 into next st] twice (36)
Rnd 5 (sc2, sc2 into next st) 12 times (48)
Rnd 6 (sc3, sc2 into next st) 12 times (60)
Rnd 7 sc2 into each st (120)
Rnd 8 sc
Sew starting chain together to close.
Fold over one short edge and sew to secure, then attach to underside of body with fold at front.

RHINOPHORES (make two)
Ch13, turn and work back down ch as follows:
sl st3, hdc3, dc6.

Finish by sewing eyes into place with Black yarn.

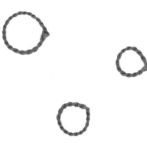

HERMIT CRAB

HEAD SEGMENT

Begin by sc6 into ring.

Rnd 1 (sc2 into next st) 6 times (12 sts)
Rnd 2 (sc1, sc2 into next st) 6 times (18)
Rnds 3–9 sc (7 rnds)
Rnd 10 [(sc2tog) twice, sc2] 3 times (12)
Rnds 11–13 sc (3 rnds)
Rnd 14 (sc2tog, sc2) 3 times (9)
Rnd 15 (sc2tog, sc1) 3 times (6)

TAIL SEGMENT

Begin by sc6 into ring.

Rnd 1 (sc2 into next st) 6 times (12)
Rnd 2 (sc1, sc2 into next st) 6 times (18)
Rnds 3–5 sc (3 rnds)
Rnd 6 (sc2tog, sc4) 3 times (15)
Rnds 7–10 sc (4 rnds)
Rnd 11 sc2tog, sc13 (14)
Rnd 12 sc2tog, sc12 (13)
Rnd 13 sc2tog, sc11 (12)
Rnd 14 sc2tog, sc10 (11)
Rnd 15 sc
Rnd 16 sc2tog, sc9 (10)
Rnd 17 sc2tog, sc8 (9)
Rnd 18 sc2tog, sc7 (8)
Rnds 19–21 sc (3 rnds)
Rnd 22 sc2tog, sc4, sc2tog (6)
Rnds 23–25 sc (3 rnds)

LARGE CLAW (right)

Ch6 and sl st to join into a circle.

Rnds 1–7 sc (7 rnds)
Rnd 8 (sc2 into next st) 6 times (12)
Rnd 9 (sc2 into next st) 12 times (24)
Rnds 10–14 sc (5 rnds)

Count back 8 sts and sc into this st from the RS of the fabric to split off the last 8 sts into a separate round and work as follows:

Rnds 1–4 sc (4 rnds)
Rnd 5 sc2, (sc2tog) twice, sc2 (6)
Rnd 6 sc2, sc2tog, sc2 (5)
Rnd 7 sc1, sc2tog, sc2 (4)

Rejoin and work remaining 16 sts as follows:

Rnds 1–6 sc (6 rnds)
Rnd 7 sc3, (sc1, sc2tog) 3 times, sc4 (13)
Rnd 8 sc3, (sc2tog) 3 times, sc4 (10)
Rnd 9 sc2, (sc2tog) twice, sc4 (8)
Rnd 10 sc2, (sc2tog) twice, sc2 (6)

SMALL CLAW (left)

Ch6 and sl st to join into a circle.

Rnds 1–3 sc (3 rnds)
Rnd 4 (sc2 into next st) 6 times (12)
Rnd 5 (sc1, sc2 into next st) 6 times (18)
Rnds 6–7 sc (2 rnds)

Count back 6 sts and sc into this st from the RS of the fabric to split off the last 6 sts into a separate round and work as follows:

Rnds 1–3 sc (3 rnds)
Rnd 4 (sc2tog) 3 times (3)

Rejoin and work remaining 12 sts as follows:

Rnds 1–4 sc (4 rnds)

Rnd 5 sc4, (sc2tog) twice, sc4 (10)
Rnd 6 sc2, (sc2tog) 3 times, sc2 (7)

Attach head segment to tail segment and then roll
end of tail into shape and sew to secure. Sew claws
into position.

LEGS (make eight)
Add four pairs of legs working SLIP STITCH CHAINS (see
page 22) along each side of head and tail, starting
closest to the claws.
Long legs (make two pairs)
Sl st into side of head segment.
Ch15 and work back down ch as follows: sl st4, sc4, hdc6.

Medium legs (make one pair)
Sl st into side of head segment.
Ch13 and work back down ch as follows: sl st4, sc4, hdc4.
Short legs (make one pair)
Sl st into side of tail segment.
Ch5 and work back down ch as follows: sc4.

EYE STALKS (make two)
Work two ch5 slip stitch chains into eye position.

Finish by sewing eyes into place with Black yarn.

SEAHORSE

TAIL/BODY/HEAD
Begin by sc4 into ring.
Rnds 1–15 sc (15 rnds)
Rnd 16 sc2 into next st, sc3 (5 sts)
Rnds 17–19 sc (3 rnds)
Rnd 20 sc2 into next st, sc4 (6)
Rnds 21–23 sc (3 rnds)
Rnd 24 sc2 into next st, sc5 (7)
Rnds 25–27 sc (3 rnds)
Rnd 28 sc2 into next st, sc6 (8)
Rnds 29–31 sc (3 rnds)
Rnd 32 sc2 into next st, sc7 (9)
Rnds 33–34 sc (2 rnds)
Rnd 35 sc2 into next st, sc8 (10)
Rnd 36 (sc2 into next st, sc4) twice (12)
Rnd 37 (sc2 into next st, sc5) twice (14)
Rnd 38 (sc2 into next st) 4 times, sc10 (18)
Rnd 39 sc
Rnd 40 sc3, (sc2 into next st) twice, sc13 (20)
Rnd 41 sc
Rnd 42 sc4, (sc2 into next st) twice, sc14 (22)
Rnd 43 sc5, (sc2 into next st) twice, sc15 (24)
Rnds 44–48 sc (5 rnds)
Rnd 49 (sc4, sc2tog) 4 times (20)
Rnd 50 (sc3, sc2tog) 4 times (16)
Rnd 51 (sc2, sc2tog) 4 times (12)
Rnd 52 sc3, (sc2tog) 3 times, sc3 (9)
Rnd 53 sc3, sl st3, sc3
Rnd 54 hdc2, sc1, sl st3, sc1, hdc2
Rnd 55 (hdc2 into next st) twice, sc1, sl st3, sc1, (hdc2 into next st) twice (13)
Rnd 56 (hdc2 into next st) 3 times, sl st6, hdc1, (hdc2 into next st) 3 times (19)
Rnd 57 dc6, hdc1, sc2, sl st6, sc2, hdc1, dc1
Rnd 58 (dc2 into next st) 3 times, dc2, hdc2, sc7, hdc3, (sc2 into next st) twice (24)
Rnd 59 (sc2tog) 4 times, sc16 (20)
Rnd 60 sc2tog, sc1, sc2tog, sc10, sc2tog, sc1, sc2tog (16)
Rnd 61 (sc2tog) twice, sc4, (sc2 into next st) twice, sc6 (16)
Rnd 62 sc2tog, sc12, sc2tog (14)
Rnd 63 sc2tog, sc10, sc2tog (12)
Rnd 64 (sc2tog, sc1) 4 times (8)
Rnds 65–70 sc (6 rnds)
Rnd 71 (sc1, sc2 into next st) 4 times (12)
Stuff body and head and then sew nose closed around the inside of Rnd 69.

FLIPPERS (make two)
Ch8, turn and work back down ch as follows:
Row 1 miss 2 sts, dc2, hdc2, sc2
Row 2 ch1, turn, sc2, hdc2, dc2

FRILL
Work two rows of ch5 CHAIN LOOPS (see page 67) up the back of the neck and head.

Finish by sewing eyes into place with Black yarn.

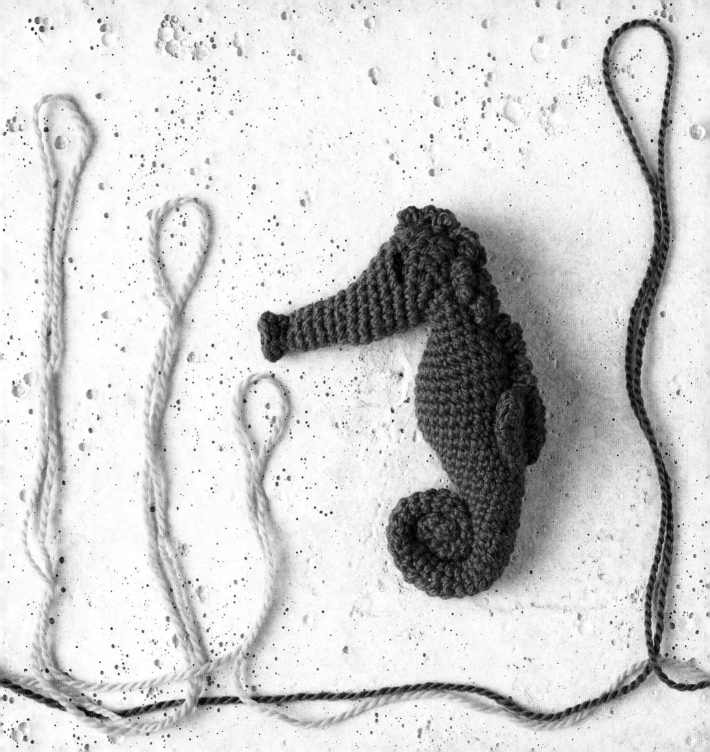

CHAIN LOOPS

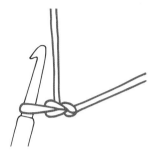

1 Insert the hook through the fabric at the desired
   position, yarn over, and pull through the fabric.

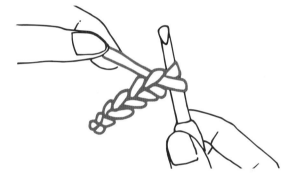

2 Chain the number of stitches stated in the pattern.

3 Attach the chain to the fabric with a slip stitch
   approximately two stitches or two rounds away from
   the start of the chain. Repeat until the required area
   is covered.

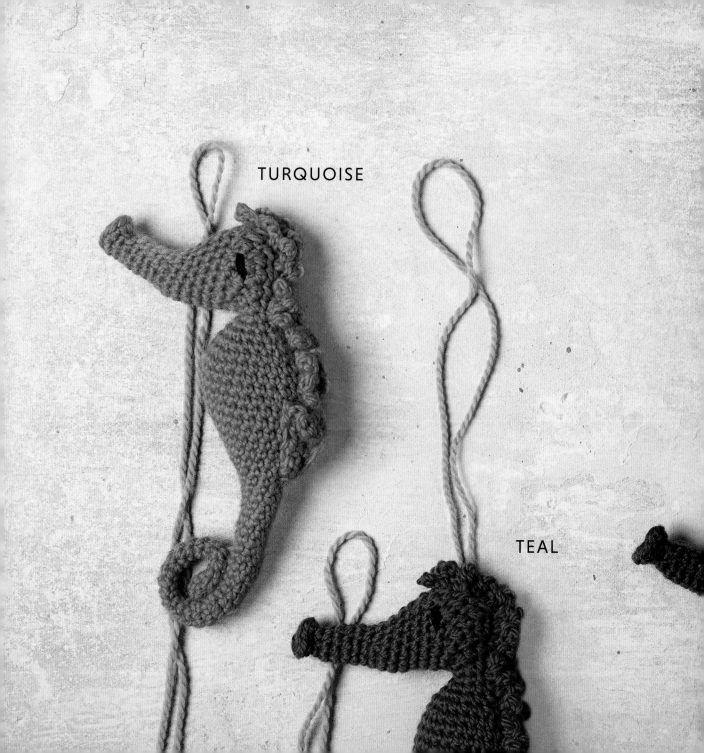

TURQUOISE

TEAL

AMETHYST

MAGENTA

RUBY

PRAWN

HEAD/BODY
Begin by sc6 into ring.
Rnd 1 sc
Rnd 2 (sc2, sc2 into next st) twice (8 sts)
Rnd 3 (sc3, sc2 into next st) twice (10)
Rnd 4 (sc4, sc2 into next st) twice (12)
Rnds 5–6 sc (2 rnds)
Rnd 7 (sc1, sc2 into next st) 3 times, sc6 (15)
Rnds 8–10 sc (3 rnds)
Work into back loops only.
Rnds 11–12 sc (2 rnds)
Work as normal (through whole stitch).
Rnd 13 sc4, sc2tog, sc1, sc2tog, sc4, sc2 into next st, sc1 (14)
Rnd 14 sc3, (sc2tog) twice, sc4, sc2 into next st, sc2 (13)
Work into back loops only.
Rnd 15 sc
Rnd 16 sc3, (sc2tog) twice, sc3, sc2 into next st, sc2 (12)
Work as normal (through whole stitch).
Rnd 17 sc1, sc2tog, sc2, sc2tog, sc5 (10)
Rnd 18 sc2, (sc2tog) twice, sc2, sc2 into next st, sc1 (9)
Rnd 19 sc1, (sc2tog) twice, sc2, sc2 into next st, sc1 (8)
Rnd 20 sc1, (sc2tog) twice, sc3 (6)
Rnds 21–22 sc (2 rnds)
Stuff and continue to tail.

TAIL
Ch8, turn and work back down ch as follows:
skip 2 sts, dc2, hdc1, sc2, sl st into base to secure.
Repeat twice more.

WALKING LEGS (make ten)
Work five pairs of ch9 SLIP STITCH CHAINS (see page 22)
   along underside of body.

SWIMMING LEGS (make ten)
Work five 1¼ inches (3 cm) KNOT LENGTHS (see page 73)
   along underside of tail.

ANTENNAE (make two)
Work one 12½ inches (32 cm) knot length under head.

Finish by sewing eyes into place with Black yarn.

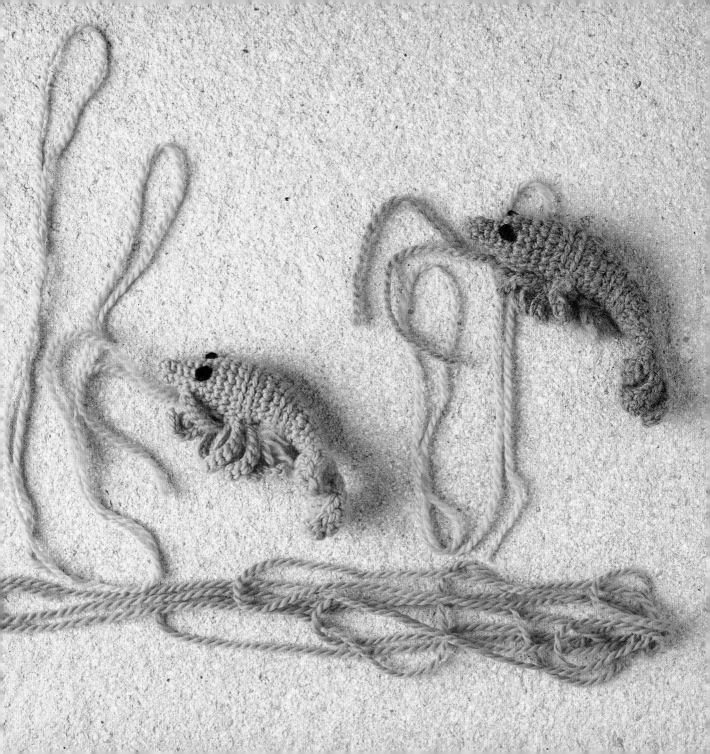

KNOTTING ON LENGTHS

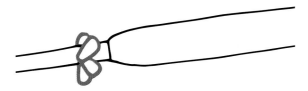

1 Insert the hook through the fabric around a stitch.

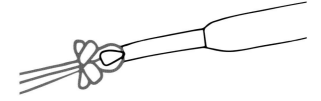

2 Yarn over with the middle of a length of yarn (or several held together) and pull through the stitch to form a loop.

3 Thread the ends of the yarn through the loop and pull to tighten to the fabric. Trim if necessary.

PELICAN

BODY/HEAD
Working in Cream, begin by sc6 into ring.
Rnd 1 (sc2 into next st) 6 times (12 sts)
Rnd 2 (sc1, sc2 into next st) 6 times (18)
Rnd 3 (sc2, sc2 into next st) 6 times (24)
Rnd 4 (sc3, sc2 into next st) 6 times (30)
Rnds 5–12 sc (8 rnds)
Rnd 13 (sc3, sc2tog) 6 times (24)
Rnd 14 (sc2tog) 12 times (12)
Rnd 15 (sc2tog) 6 times (6)
Rnds 16–18 sc (3 rnds)
Rnd 19 (sc2 into next st) 6 times (12)
Rnd 20 (sc2 into next st) 12 times (24)
Rnd 21 (sc3, sc2 into next st) 6 times (30)
Rnds 22–24 sc (3 rnds)
Rnd 25 (sc3, sc2tog) 6 times (24)
Rnd 26 (sc2, sc2tog) 6 times (18)
Rnd 27 (sc1, sc2tog) 6 times (12)
Rnd 28 (sc2tog) 6 times (6)

LEGS (make two)
Working in Yellow, ch5 and sl st to join into a circle.
Rnds 1–4 sc (4 rnds)
Rnd 5 (sc2 into next st) 5 times (10)
Rnd 6 sc
Rnd 7 (sc4, sc2 into next st) twice (12)
Rnd 8 (sc5, sc2 into next st) twice (14)
Rnd 9 (sc6, sc2 into next st) twice (16)
Rnd 10 sc
Fold flat and sc across edge to close.
Do not stuff.

WINGS (make two)
Working in Cream, begin by sc6 into ring.
Rnd 1 (sc2 into next st) 6 times (12)
Rnd 2 sc
Rnd 3 (sc4, sc2tog) twice (10)
Rnd 4 (sc3, sc2tog) twice (8)
Rnd 5 (sc2, sc2tog) twice (6)
Rnd 6 (sc1, sc2tog) twice (4)
Do not stuff.

BEAK
Working in Yellow, begin by sc6 into ring.
Rnd 1 (sc2 into next st) 6 times (12)
Rnds 2–7 sc (6 rnds)
Rnd 8 (sc2 into next st, sc1) twice (incomplete rnd)
Count back 6 sts and sc into this st from the RS of the
    fabric to split off the last 6 sts you have worked
    into a separate round.
Rnds 1–6 sc (6 rnds)
Rnd 7 (sc2tog) 3 times (3)

TAIL
Working in Cream, work three ch5 SLIP STITCH CHAINS
    (see page 22) into tail position.

CREST
Working in Cream, work three ch5 slip stitch chains
    into top of head.

Finish by sewing eyes into place with Black yarn.

RAY

HEAD/BODY

Ch18 and sl st to join into a circle.

Rnd 1 sc

Rnd 2 sc3, (sc2 into next st) 3 times, sc6, (sc2 into next st) 3 times, sc3 (24 sts)

Rnd 3 sc

Rnd 4 sc5, (sc2 into next st) twice, sc10, (sc2 into next st) twice, sc5 (28)

Rnd 5 sc

Rnd 6 sc6, (sc2 into next st) twice, sc12, (sc2 into next st) twice, sc6 (32)

Rnd 7 sc

Rnd 8 sc6, (sc2 into next st) 4 times, sc12, (sc2 into next st) 4 times, sc6 (40)

Rnd 9 sc

Rnd 10 sc9, sc2 into next st, sc20, sc2 into next st, sc9 (42)

Rnd 11 sc

Rnd 12 sc10, (sc2 into next st) 3 times, sc16, (sc2 into next st) 3 times, sc10 (48)

Rnd 13 sc11, sc2 into next st, sc24, sc2 into next st, sc11 (50)

Rnd 14 sc

Rnd 15 sc1 (incomplete rnd)

Continue to tail.

TAIL

Fold flat and continue working through both edges of body.

Ch3, tr1, dc1, hdc1, sc5

Next, working along one edge of body only, sc8, cross to other edge of body, sc8 to form 16-st rnd and work as follows:

Rnd 1 (sc2, sc2tog) 4 times (12)

Rnd 2 (sc1, sc2tog) 4 times (8)

Rnd 3 sc

Rnd 4 (sc2, sc2tog) twice (6)

Rnds 5–7 sc (3 rnds)

Rnd 8 (sc1, sc2tog) twice (4)

Rnds 9–10 sc (2 rnds)

Next, ch12 and sl st back down ch

Rejoin at base of tail and continue working through both edges of body on opposite side.

Sc5, hdc1, dc1, tr1, ch3, sl st to secure.

CEPHALIC LOBES

Stuff and fold head flat.

Rejoin yarn and ch6, sc5 down chain, sc7 across head, ch6, sc5 down chain.

Finish by sewing eyes into place with Black yarn.

TREBLE CROCHET STITCH (TR)

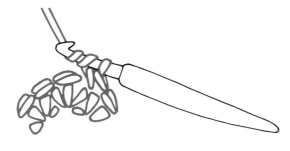

1 Yarn over twice and insert the hook into the next stitch.

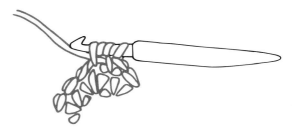

2 Yarn over and pull through the stitch (four loops on hook).

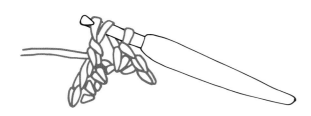

3 Yarn over and pull through the first two loops on the hook (three loops on hook), then repeat and pull through the first two loops each time until only loop remains on the hook.

SHARK

HEAD/BODY/TAIL

Begin by sc6 into ring.

Rnd 1 (sc1, sc2 into next st) 3 times (9 sts)

Rnd 2 sc2 into next st, sc2, sc2 into next st, sc5 (11)

Rnd 3 sc

Rnd 4 sc2 into next st, sc3, (sc2 into next st) twice, sc4, sc2 into next st (15)

Rnd 5 sc

Rnd 6 sc7, sc2 into next st, sc6, sc2 into next st (17)

Rnd 7 sc2 into next st, (sc3, sc2 into next st) 4 times (22)

Rnd 8 sc9, (sc2 into next st, sc5) twice, sc2 into next st (25)

Rnd 9 sc

Rnd 10 (sc4, sc2 into next st) 5 times (30)

Rnds 11–13 sc (3 rnds)

Rnd 14 sc14, sc2tog, sc5, sc2tog, sc5, sc2tog (27)

Rnd 15 sc13, sc2tog, sc4, sc2tog, sc4, sc2tog (24)

Rnd 16 sc14, sc2tog, sc2, sc2tog, sc2, sc2tog (21)

Rnd 17 sc2tog, sc5, sc2tog, sc5, sc2tog, sc5 (18)

Rnd 18 (sc4, sc2tog) 3 times (15)

Rnd 19 (sc3, sc2tog) 3 times (12)

Rnds 20–21 sc (2 rnds)

Rnd 22 (sc1, sc2tog) 4 times (8)

Stuff and continue.

Rnds 23–24 sc (2 rnds)

Next, sc3, then ch6 and sl st halfway across to the other side of rnd to form two 10-st rnds (4 from rnd, 6 on chain).

Work each rnd as follows:

Rnds 1–2 sc (2 rnds)

Rnd 3 (sc2tog, sc3) twice (8)

Rnd 4 sc

Rnd 5 (sc2tog, sc2) twice (6)

PECTORAL FINS (make two)

Begin by sc6 into ring.

Rnds 1–3 sc (3 rnds)

Do not stuff.

DORSAL FIN

Begin by sc5 into ring.

Rnd 1 sc4, sc2 into next st (6)

Rnd 2 sc5, sc2 into next st (7)

Rnd 3 sc6, sc2 into next st (8)

Rnd 4 sc7, sc2 into next st (9)

Rnd 5 sc8, sc2 into next st (10)

Do not stuff.

Finish by sewing eyes into place with Black yarn.

BLUE WHALE

HEAD/BODY/TAIL

Ch4

Rnd 1 sc2, sc2 into next st along one side of chain, sc2, sc2 into next st along other side of chain (8 sts)

Rnd 2 (sc2 into next st, sc3) twice (10)

Rnd 3 (sc2 into next st, sc4) twice (12)

Rnd 4 (sc5, sc2 into next st) twice (14)

Rnd 5 (sc6, sc2 into next st) twice (16)

Rnd 6 sc6, (sc2 into next st, sc1) twice, sc6 (18)

Rnd 7 (sc2, sc2 into next st) 6 times (24)

Rnds 8–12 sc (5 rnds)

Rnd 13 sc12, sc2tog, sc4, sc2tog, sc4 (22)

Rnds 14–15 sc (2 rnds)

Rnd 16 sc12, sc2tog, sc2, sc2tog, sc4 (20)

Rnds 17–18 sc (2 rnds)

Rnd 19 sc12, (sc2tog) twice, sc4 (18)

Rnds 20–21 sc (2 rnds)

Rnd 22 (sc4, sc2tog) 3 times (15)

Rnd 23 sc13, sc2tog (14)

Rnd 24 sc12, sc2tog (13)

Rnd 25 sc11, sc2tog (12)

Rnd 26 sc10, sc2tog (11)

Rnd 27 sc9, sc2tog (10)

Rnds 28–29 sc (2 rnds)

Stuff and continue.

Next, sc2, then ch5 and sl st halfway across to the other side of rnd to form two 10-st rnds (5 from rnd, 5 on chain).

Work each rnd as follows:

Rnds 1–2 sc (2 rnds)

Rnd 3 sc2tog, sc8 (9)

Rnd 4 sc2tog, sc7 (8)

Rnd 5 sc2tog, sc6 (7)

Stuff and continue.

Rnd 6 sc2tog, sc5 (6)

Rnd 7 sc2tog, sc4 (5)

FLIPPERS (make two)

Sl st into position on body.

Ch6, turn and work back down ch as follows:

sc2, hdc1, dc2, sl st into body to secure.

DORSAL FIN

Work one ch3 SLIP STITCH CHAIN (see page 22) into position on top of body.

Finish by sewing eyes into place with Black yarn.

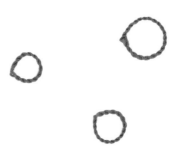

NARWHAL

HEAD/BODY/TAIL

Working in Shale, begin by sc6 into ring.

Rnd 1 (sc2 into next st) 6 times (12 sts)

Rnd 2 (sc1, sc2 into next st) 6 times (18)

Rnd 3 (sc2, sc2 into next st) 6 times (24)

Rnd 4 [sc4, (sc2 into next st) twice] 4 times (32)

Rnds 5–16 sc (12 rnds)

Rnd 17 (sc1, sc2tog) 3 times, sc11, (sc1, sc2tog) 4 times (25)

Rnd 18 sc

Rnd 19 (sc1, sc2tog) twice, sc10, (sc1, sc2tog) 3 times (20)

Rnd 20 sc

Rnd 21 sc2tog, sc18 (19)

Rnd 22 sc2tog, sc17 (18)

Rnd 23 (sc2tog, sc7) twice (16)

Rnd 24 (sc2, sc2tog) 4 times (12)

Rnd 25 (sc2tog, sc4) twice (10)

Rnds 26–29 sc (4 rnds)

Next, ch7 and sl st halfway across to the other side of rnd to form two 12-st rnds (5 from rnd, 7 on chain).

Work each rnd as follows:

Rnds 1–2 sc (2 rnds)

Rnd 3 (sc1, sc2tog) 4 times (8)

Rnds 4–5 sc (2 rnds)

Stuff and continue.

Rnd 6 (sc2tog) 4 times (4)

FINS (make two)

Working in Shale, begin by sc6 into ring.

Rnds 1–3 sc (3 rnds)

Do not stuff.

TUSK

Working in Silver, ch6 and sl st to join into a circle.

Rnds 1–8 sc (8 rnds)

Rnd 9 sc2tog, sc4 (5)

Rnd 10 sc2tog, sc3 (4)

Do not stuff.

Finish by sewing eyes into place with Black yarn.

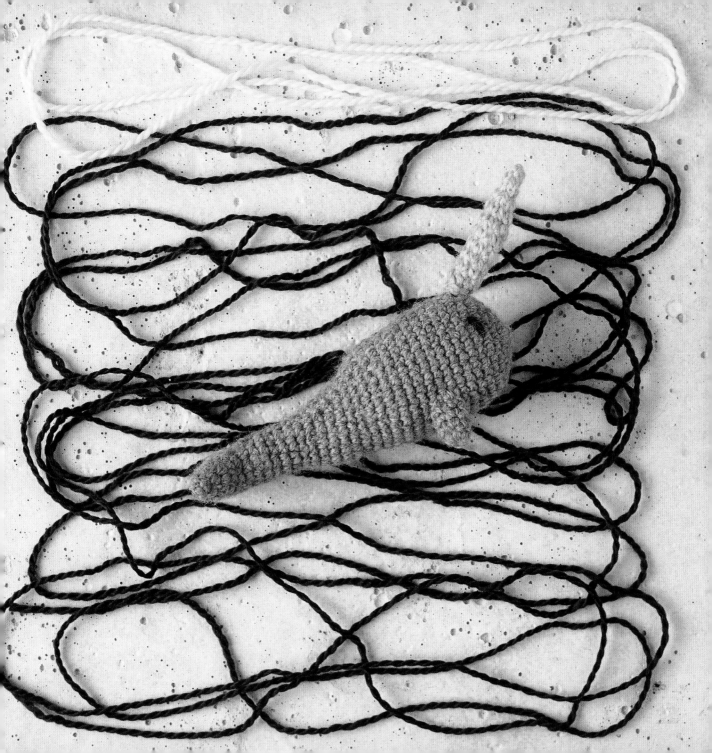

THE NEXT STEP: CHANGING COLOR

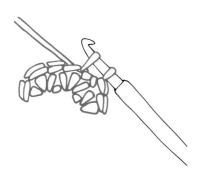  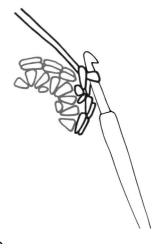

1 Insert the hook through the next stitch, yarn over, and pull through the stitch (two loops on hook).

2 Yarn over, with the new color and complete the single crochet stitch with this new yarn.

3 Continue with this new yarn, leaving the original yarn at the back of the work. Cut the original yarn if this is a one-off color change, or run it along the back of the fabric if returning to it later.

You work this color change at the end of the stitch BEFORE the first stitch in the new color.

SEA SNAKE

TAIL/BODY/HEAD

Working in Black, begin by sc4 into ring.
Rnds 1–6 sc (6 rnds)
Rnd 7 sc2 into next st, sc3 (5 sts)
Change to Cream.
Rnds 8–13 sc (6 rnds)
Rnd 14 sc2 into next st, sc4 (6)
Change to Black.
Rnds 15–20 sc (6 rnds)
Rnd 21 sc2 into next st, sc5 (7)
Change to Cream.
Rnds 22–27 sc (6 rnds)
Change to Black.
Rnd 28 sc2 into next st, sc6 (8)
Rnds 29–33 sc (5 rnds)
Change to Cream.
Rnds 34–38 sc (5 rnds)
Rnd 39 sc2 into next st, sc7 (9)
Change to Black.
Rnds 40–45 sc (6 rnds)
Change to Cream.
Rnds 46–49 sc (4 rnds)
Rnd 50 sc2 into next st, sc8 (10)
Change to Black.
Rnds 51–55 sc (5 rnds)
Change to Cream.
Rnds 56–60 sc (5 rnds)
Change to Black.
Rnd 61 sc2 into next st, sc9 (11)
Rnds 62–65 sc (4 rnds)
Change to Cream.
Rnds 66–70 sc (5 rnds)

Change to Black.
Rnd 71 sc
Rnd 72 sc2 into next st, sc10 (12)
Rnds 73–74 sc (2 rnds)
Change to Cream.
Rnds 75–78 sc (4 rnds)
Change to Black.
Rnds 79–82 sc (4 rnds)
Change to Cream.
Rnds 83–86 sc (4 rnds)
Continue in 3 rnds Black, 3 rnds Cream pattern.
Rnds 87–130 sc (44 rnds)
Rnd 131 (sc2tog, sc4) twice (10)
Rnd 132 sc
Rnd 133 (sc2 into next st) 6 times, sc4 (16)
Change to Cream.
Rnd 134 (sc1, sc2 into next st) 6 times, sc4 (22)
Rnds 135–137 sc (3 rnds)
Rnd 138 sc3, (sc2tog) 8 times, sc3 (14)
Rnds 139–141 sc (3 rnds)
Rnd 142 (sc2tog) 7 times (7)

Finish by sewing eyes and nostrils into place with Black yarn.

With this pattern, stuff as you go along to avoid quite a fiddly job at the end of the project.

HAMMERHEAD SHARK

COLORS | STEEL, CHARCOAL

HEAD/BODY/TAIL

Working in Steel, ch13.

Rnd 1 sc2 into next st, sc10, sc2 into next st along one side of chain, sc2 into next st, sc10, sc2 into next st along other side of chain (28 sts)

Rnds 2–5 sc (4 rnds)

Rnd 6 (sc2tog) twice, sc6, (sc2tog) 4 times, sc6, (sc2tog) twice (20)

Rnd 7 (sc2tog) 10 times (10)

Rnd 8 sc

Rnd 9 (sc4, sc2 into next st) twice (12)

Rnd 10 sc

Rnd 11 (sc3, sc2 into next st) 3 times (15)

Rnds 12–13 sc (2 rnds)

Rnd 14 (sc2 into next st, sc4) 3 times (18)

Rnds 15–17 sc (3 rnds)

Rnd 18 (sc2 into next st, sc5) 3 times (21)

Rnd 19 sc

Rnd 20 (sc2 into next st, sc6) 3 times (24)

Rnd 21 sc

Rnd 22 (sc2 into next st, sc7) 3 times (27)

Rnds 23–24 sc (2 rnds)

Rnd 25 (sc5, sc2tog, sc2) 3 times (24)

Rnd 26 (sc4, sc2tog, sc2) 3 times (21)

Rnd 27 (sc3, sc2tog, sc2) 3 times (18)

Rnds 28–29 sc (2 rnds)

Rnd 30 (sc2tog, sc4) 3 times (15)

Rnds 31–32 sc (2 rnds)

Rnd 33 (sc2tog, sc3) 3 times (12)

Rnds 34–35 sc (2 rnds)

Rnd 36 (sc2tog, sc2) 3 times (9)

Rnds 37–39 sc (3 rnds)

Rnd 40 (sc2tog, sc1) 3 times (6)

Stuff and continue.

Next, ch6 and sl st halfway across to the other side of rnd to form two 9-st rnds (3 from rnd, 6 on chain).

Work top 9-st rnd as follows:

Rnds 1–2 sc (2 rnds)

Rnd 3 sc2tog, sc7 (8)

Rnd 4 sc

Rnd 5 sc2tog, sc6 (7)

Rnd 6 sc

Change to Charcoal.

Rnd 7 sc

Stuff and continue.

Rnd 8 sc2tog, sc5 (6)

Rnd 9 sc2tog, sc2, sc2tog (4)

Rejoin Steel and work bottom 9-st rnd as follows:

Rnd 1 sc

Rnd 2 sc2tog, sc7 (8)

Rnd 3 sc2tog, sc6 (7)

Rnd 4 sc2tog, sc5 (6)

Rnd 5 sc2tog, sc4 (5)

Rnd 6 sc2tog, sc3 (4)

DORSAL FIN

Working in Steel, ch12 and sl st to join into a circle.

Rnd 1 sc

Rnd 2 sc2tog, sc10 (11)

Rnd 3 sc2tog, sc9 (10)

Rnd 4 sc2tog, sc8 (9)

Rnd 5 sc2tog, sc7 (8)

Change to Charcoal.

Rnd 6 (sc2tog, sc2) twice (6)

Rnd 7 sc

Rnd 8 (sc2tog, sc2) twice (4)

Do not stuff.

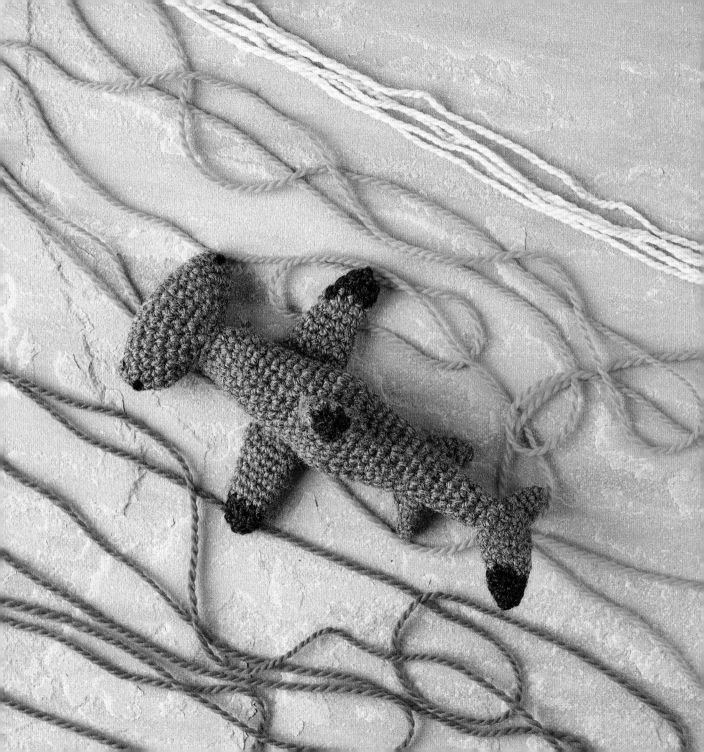

PECTORAL FINS (make two)

Working in Steel, ch12 and sl st to
  join into a circle.

Rnd 1 sc

Rnd 2 sc2tog, sc10 (11)

Rnd 3 sc

Rnd 4 sc2tog, sc9 (10)

Rnd 5 sc

Rnd 6 sc2tog, sc8 (9)

Rnd 7 sc

Change to Charcoal.

Rnd 8 sc

Rnd 9 sc2tog, sc7 (8)

Rnd 10 (sc2tog, sc2) (6)

Do not stuff.

PELVIC FINS (make two)

Working in Steel, ch8 and sl st to
  join into a circle.

Rnds 1–2 sc (2 rnds)

Rnd 3 (sc2tog, sc2) twice (6)

Rnd 4 sc2tog, sc4 (5)

Rnd 5 sc

Do not stuff.

Finish by sewing eyes into place with Black yarn.

CLOWNFISH

HEAD/BODY/TAIL

Working in Orange, begin by sc6 into ring.
Rnd 1 (sc1, sc2 into next st) 3 times (9 sts)
Rnd 2 (sc2, sc2 into next st) 3 times (12)
Rnd 3 (sc3, sc2 into next st) 3 times (15)
Rnd 4 (sc4, sc2 into next st) 3 times (18)
Rnd 5 (sc5, sc2 into next st) 3 times (21)
Change to Charcoal.
Rnd 6 sc
Change to Cream.
Rnd 7 (sc6, sc2 into next st) 3 times (24)
Rnd 8 sc
Change to Charcoal.
Rnd 9 sc
Change to Orange.
Rnds 10–12 sc (3 rnds)
Change to Charcoal.
Rnd 13 sc
Change to Cream.
Rnds 14–15 sc (2 rnds)
Change to Charcoal.
Rnd 16 sc
Change to Orange.
Rnds 17–18 sc (2 rnds)
Rnd 19 (sc2tog) 12 times (12)
Change to Charcoal.
Rnd 20 sc
Change to Cream.
Rnds 21–22 sc (2 rnds)
Change to Charcoal.
Rnd 23 sc
Change to Orange.
Rnd 24 sc
Stuff and continue to tail.

TAIL

Fold flat and work across edge as follows:
dc2 into first st, dc4, dc2 into last st (8).
Turn and dc8 back across.
Change to Charcoal, turn, and sc8 back across.

FINS (make five)

Work spiny dorsal fin (front top), soft dorsal fin (back top)
   and bottom back fin as follows:
Working in Orange, sl st into position then work toward
   tail, working sts into body as follows: (dc2 into next st)
   twice, dc1 (5).
Change to Charcoal, turn, and sc5 back across.
Work two pelvic fins and two pectoral fins as follows:
Working in Orange, sl st into position and dc4 into same st.
Change to Charcoal, turn, and sc4 back across.

Finish by sewing eyes into place with Black yarn.

MACKEREL

HEAD/BODY/TAIL

Working in Silver, begin by sc6 into ring.

Rnd 1 sc5, sc2 into next st (7 sts)

Rnd 2 sc2 into next st, sc6 (8)

Rnd 3 (sc2 into next st, sc3) twice (10)

Rnd 4 (sc2 into next st, sc4) twice (12)

Rnd 5 (sc2 into next st, sc5) twice (14)

Rnd 6 (sc2 into next st, sc6) twice (16)

Rnds 7–9 sc (3 rnds)

Rnd 10 sc4 Silver, sc8 Steel, sc4 Silver

Rnd 11 and all subsequent odd rnds sc Silver

Rnd 12 sc2tog, sc3 Silver, sc7 Steel, sc4 Silver (15)

Rnd 14 sc2tog, sc2 Silver, sc8 Steel, sc3 Silver (14)

Rnd 16 sc2tog, sc2 Silver, sc7 Steel, sc3 Silver (13)

Rnd 18 sc2tog, sc2 Silver, sc6 Steel, sc3 Silver (12)

Rnd 20 sc4 Silver, sc5 Steel, sc3 Silver

Rnd 22 (sc2tog) twice Silver, sc2, sc2tog, sc1 Steel, sc3 Silver (9)

Rnd 24 sc7, sc2tog Silver (8)

Rnd 25 (sc2tog, sc2) twice Silver (6)

Stuff and continue.

Change to Steel.

Next, ch3 and sl st halfway across to the other side of rnd to form two 6-st rnds (3 from rnd, 3 on chain).

Work each rnd as follows:

Rnds 1–2 sc (2 rnds)

Rnd 3 sc2tog, sc4 (5)

Rnd 4 sc

Rnd 5 sc2tog, sc3 (4)

PECTORAL FINS (make two)

Working in Steel, sl st into position.

Ch4, turn and work back down ch as follows:
hdc1, sc1, sl st1.

DORSAL FIN

Working in Steel, sl st into position in direction of tail.

Ch5, turn and work back down ch as follows:
tr1, dc1, hdc1, sl st1.

REAR FIN

Working in Steel, work 3 SLIP STITCH TRAVERSE sts (see page 35) into tail position, turn and work along sts as follows: sc2, sl st1.

Finish by sewing eyes and mouth into place with Black yarn.

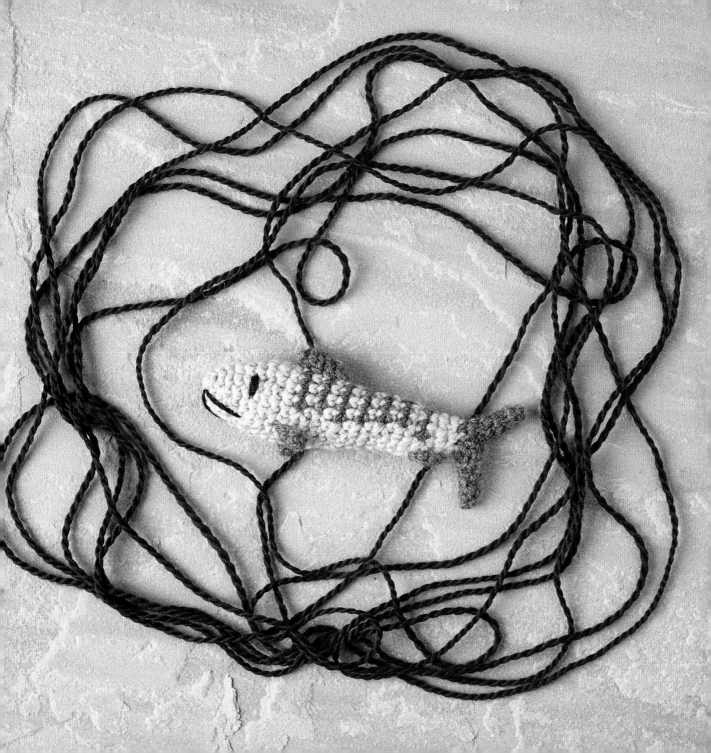

PENGUIN

BODY/HEAD

Working in Silver, begin by sc6 into ring.

Rnd 1 (sc2 into next st) 6 times (12 sts)

Rnd 2 (sc1, sc2 into next st) 6 times (18)

Rnd 3 (sc2, sc2 into next st) 6 times (24)

Rnd 4 (sc3, sc2 into next st) 6 times (30)

Rnds 5–12 sc (8 rnds)

Rnd 13 (sc3, sc2tog) 6 times (24)

Rnd 14 (sc2tog) 12 times (12)

Rnd 15 (sc2tog) 6 times (6)

Change to Charcoal.

Rnd 16 (sc2 into next st) 6 times (12)

Rnd 17 (sc2 into next st) 3 times Charcoal, (sc2 into next st) 6 times Cream, (sc2 into next st) 3 times Charcoal (24)

Rnd 18 sc3, sc2 into next st, sc2 Charcoal, sc1, sc2 into next st, (sc3, sc2 into next st) twice, sc2 Cream, sc1, sc2 into next st, sc3, sc2 into next st Charcoal (30)

Rnd 19 sc7 Charcoal, sc6 Cream, sc3 Charcoal, sc6 Cream, sc8 Charcoal

Rnds 20–21 sc7 Charcoal, sc7 Cream, sc3 Charcoal, sc6 Cream, sc7 Charcoal (2 rnds)

Rnd 22 sc3, sc2tog, sc3 Charcoal, sc2tog, sc1, sc2tog Cream, sc5 Charcoal, sc2tog, sc1, sc2tog Cream, sc2, sc2tog, sc3 Charcoal (24)

Continue in Charcoal.

Rnd 23 (sc2, sc2tog) 6 times (18)

Rnd 24 (sc1, sc2tog) 6 times (12)

Rnd 25 (sc2tog) 6 times (6)

WINGS (make two)

Working in Silver, begin by sc6 into ring.

Rnd 1 sc

Rnd 2 (sc2 into next st) 3 times, sc3 (9)

Rnds 3–4 sc (2 rnds)

Rnd 5 (sc2, sc2 into next st) 3 times (12)

Rnds 6–7 sc (2 rnds)

Fold in half and sc across top.

Fold flat and sc across edge to close.

Do not stuff.

FEET (make two)

Working in Charcoal, begin by sc6 into ring.

Rnd 1 (sc1, sc2 into next st) 3 times (9)

Rnds 2–3 sc (2 rnds)

Rnd 4 (sc2, sc2 into next st) 3 times (12)

Rnds 5–6 sc (2 rnds)

Fold flat and sc across edge to close.

Do not stuff.

BEAK

Working in Charcoal, begin by sc4 into ring.

Rnds 1–2 sc (2 rnds)

Rnd 3 (sc2tog) twice (2)

Do not stuff.

Finish by sewing eyes into place with Black yarn.

CONCH SHELL

SHELL

Begin by sc6 into ring.

Working into back loops only (including making bobble):

Rnd 1 (MB, sc2 into next st) 3 times (9 sts) (makes 3 bobbles)

Rnd 2 (sc2, sc2 into next st) 3 times (12)

Rnd 3 (sc1, sc2 into next st) 6 times (18)

Rnd 4 (sc1, MB, sc2 into next st) 6 times (24) (makes 6 bobbles)

Rnd 5 (sc3, sc2 into next st) 6 times (30)

Rnd 6 (sc4, sc2 into next st) 6 times (36)

Rnd 7 (sc2, MB) 12 times (makes 12 bobbles)

Rnd 8 sc

Rnd 9 (sc5, sc2 into next st) 6 times (42)

Rnd 10 sc

Continue the next section in rows as normal (through whole stitch).

Row 1 (WS) turn, sc42

Row 2 (RS) turn, sc42

Row 3 (WS) turn, sc42

Row 4 (RS) turn, (sc5, sc2tog) 6 times (36)

Row 5 (WS) turn, sc36

Row 6 (RS) turn, (sc4, sc2tog) 6 times (30)

Row 7 (WS) turn, sc30

Row 8 (RS) turn, (sc3, sc2tog) 6 times (24)

Row 9 (WS) turn, sc24

Row 10 (RS) turn, sc24

Row 11 (WS) turn, sc24

Row 12 (RS) turn, (sc6, sc2tog) 3 times (21)

Row 13 (WS) turn, sc21

Row 14 (RS) turn, (sc5, sc2tog) 3 times (18)

Row 15 (WS) turn, sc18

Row 16 (RS) turn, (sc4, sc2tog) 3 times (15)

Row 17 (WS) turn, sc15

Row 18 (RS) turn, sc15

Row 19 (WS) turn, sc15

Row 20 (RS) turn, (sc3, sc2tog) 3 times (12)

Row 21 (WS) turn, sc12

Row 22 (RS) turn, (sc2, sc2tog) 3 times (9)

Row 23 (WS) turn, sc9

Row 24 (RS) turn, (sc1, sc2tog) 3 times (6)

Fold end and holding edges together, sc6 along from tip up toward shell through both edges, then open outward and continue to sc into each stitch around entire remaining edge to create opening.

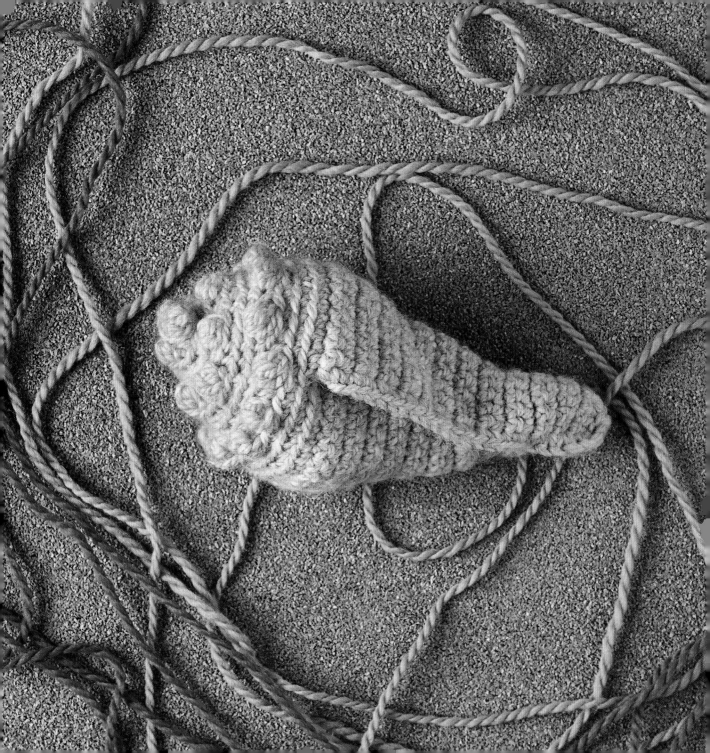

MAKE BOBBLE (MB)

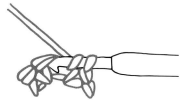 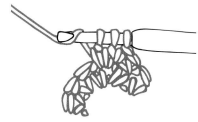 

1 Yarn over hook, insert hook into stitch, yarn over, and pull through stitch (three loops on hook). Yarn over and pull through first two loops on hook (two loops on hook).

2 Yarn over, insert hook into same stitch, yarn over, and pull through stitch (four loops on hook). Yarn over and pull through first two loops on hook (three loops on hook).

3 Yarn over, insert hook into same stitch, yarn over, and pull through stitch (five loops on hook). Yarn over and pull through first two loops on hook (four loops on hook). Yarn over and pull through all four loops.

WORKING ROWS NOT ROUNDS

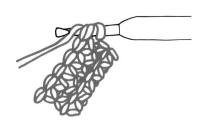 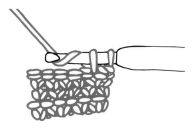

1 Work across the stated number of stitches as instructed.

2 Turn and work back into the last stitch of the previous row.

OTHER BOOKS IN THE SERIES

These mini Edward's Menagerie animal patterns are part of a wider collection of animal crochet projects. In the whole range, there are now over five hundred different animal patterns.

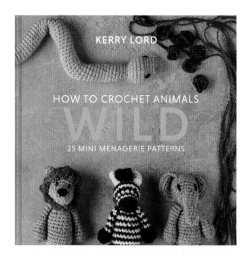

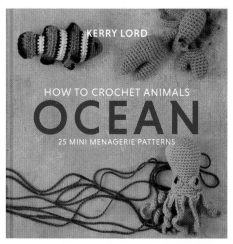

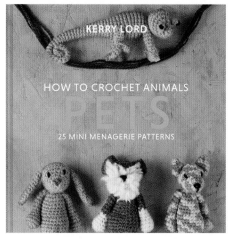

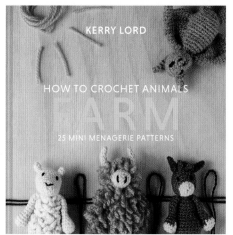

This sloth pattern can be found in *How to Crochet Animals: Wild.*

BE SOCIAL

One of the most exciting things about crocheting is joining the active online community that helps and inspires one another every day in their shared hobby. Share your creations using the tag #edsanimals to join in.

ON THIS PAGE

@rosebobine
@wysehannah
@emmapalin93

ON THE OPPOSITE PAGE

@weespunch
@vbirdflies
@rachelelizabeththomas
@hookmanchester
@jamesmakesthings
@bslovescrochet
@bethaucott
@abbiethart31
@miss.gemma.hughes

ANIMAL INDEX

TECHNIQUE INDEX

Please note American English crochet terms are used throughout.
Please see page 6 for more information.

ACKNOWLEDGMENTS

The exciting style in this book has only been made possible with the talented pen of Evelyn Birch, who has patiently captured my hands and hook in illustrations that will make it even easier to learn to crochet. Her assistance in the creation of this mini Edward's Menagerie series has sparked a new direction and I have thoroughly enjoyed collaborating to create such beautiful books.

Special thanks to Evelyn Birch and Rachel Critchley for quite a few rainy summer days fuelled by custard tarts, spent hooking up just one more sardine and testing patterns.

A specific thank you to TOFT team members Jo Clements, Nathasja Vermaning and Helen Wyatt for their extra neat stitches and speedy hooks that help make the lovely photography in this book possible, and Harriet Hart for her attention to detail and adding the polish. Wider thanks are due to the TOFT team (past and present) who work hard every day to deliver TOFT products around the world, and help our customers learn to crochet and enjoy the craft as much as we do. Working alongside a group of such brilliant and enthusiastic people is an honor.

Without the support of my family I could not continue to run an expanding business, so a particular thanks goes to Doug Lord and my parents in continuing to enable me to follow my dreams.

Every year Edward gets closer to gaining the coordination and concentration to be able to make his own first crochet animal. Perhaps one of these minis will be the one! My two children continue to inspire me with their constant feedback on what's flying off the end of my hook.

A final thanks to all the Edward's Menagerie fans out there who continue to support TOFT. Your passion for my designs and our yarns keeps me crocheting as fast as I can.

ABOUT THE AUTHOR

Kerry Lord is the founder of TOFT, a dynamic British yarn brand specializing in luxury wools and approachable patterns. Initially established with a focus on fashion-led knitting kits, Kerry first created the super-popular Edward's Menagerie series of books in 2012, which have encouraged and taught thousands around the world to crochet for the first time.

TOFT continues to offer a strong design collection for both knitting and croche; a commanding presence at craft shows all over the world, sold-out pattern subscription boxes (shipping internationally), and regular workshops at their Studio HQ in Warwickshire make TOFT a big part of the contemporary craft scene, both in the UK and across the world.

Kerry enjoys collaborating and cohosting ever-larger crochet events to bring new people to the craft, such as teaching 350 workshop attendees to make a whale at the Natural History Museum, London, and a touring exhibition of over 500 crochet animals that bring together the wider range of Edward's Menagerie.

Follow her on Instagram @toft_uk to see more of her adventures in crochet.

www.toftuk.com

LARK
New York

An Imprint of Sterling Publishing Co., Inc.
122 Fifth Avenue
New York, NY 10011

ISBN 978-1-4547-1133-9

Distributed in Canada by Sterling Publishing Co., Inc.
c/o Canadian Manda
Group, 664 Annette Street
Toronto, Ontario M6S 2C8, Canada

For information about custom editions, special sales, and premium and corporate purchases, please contact Sterling Special Sales at 800-805-5489 or specialsales@sterlingpublishing.com.

Manufactured in China

2 4 6 8 10 9 7 5 3 1

sterlingpublishing.com/larkcrafts

Photography by Kristy Noble

MIX
Paper from
responsible sources
FSC® C016973